DATE _____

TO _____

_____

FROM _____

_____

_____

_____

_____

_____

Promises *for* Spirit-Led Living

Smith Wigglesworth

COMPILED BY
JUDITH COUCHMAN

VINE BOOKS
SERVANT PUBLICATIONS
ANN ARBOR, MICHIGAN

Vine Books is an imprint of Servant Publications especially designed
to serve evangelical Christians.

Compiled by Judith Couchman.

Published by Servant Publications
P.O. Box 8617
Ann Arbor, Michigan 48107

Cover design and photograph: PAZ Design Group, Salem, Oregon

99 00 01 02 10 9 8 7 6 5 4 3 2 1

Printed in the United States of America
ISBN 1-56955-114-6

LIBRARY OF CONGRESS CATALOGING-IN-PUBLICATION DATA

Wigglesworth, Smith, 1859-1947.
Promises for spirit-led living / Smith Wigglesworth ; [compiled by
Judith Couchman].
    p.   cm.
ISBN 1-56955-114-6 (alk. paper)
1. Meditations.   I. Couchman, Judith, 1953-   . II. Title.
BV4832.2.W539   1999
242—dc21   99-12794
                                            CIP

Contents

*Promises From the Bible and
Smith Wigglesworth About:*

Promises About Abiding

From the Bible:

Lord, who shall abide in thy tabernacle? who shall dwell in thy holy hill?

He that walketh uprightly, and worketh righteousness, and speaketh the truth in his heart.

He that backbiteth not with his tongue, nor doeth evil to his neighbour, nor taketh up a reproach against his neighbour.

In whose eyes a vile person is condemned; but he honoureth them that fear the Lord. He that sweareth to his own hurt, and changeth not.

He that putteth not out his money to usury, nor taketh reward against the innocent. He that doeth these things shall never be moved.

PSALM 15, KJV

From Smith Wigglesworth:

The thought that has been pressing upon my mind for some time is the thought of "abiding" and the joy of being in that place where I can always count on being in the presence of power, where I know God's presence is with me, leading to a place of victory.

Let us get hold of this thought: If we keep in a certain place with God, wonderful things may happen, for we shall then be where we reach such spiritual attainment that marvels may be wrought because we are there. Then God will have His way through us.

—*The Place of Power*

Abide in God and
He will abide in you.

Promises About Abiding

From the Bible:

And I will pray the Father, and he shall give you another Comforter, that he may abide with you for ever;

Even the Spirit of truth; whom the world cannot receive, because it seeth him not, neither knoweth him: but ye know him; for he dwelleth with you, and shall be in you.

I will not leave you comfortless: I will come to you.

Yet a little while, and the world seeth me no more; but ye see me: because I live, ye shall live also.

At that day ye shall know that I am in my Father, and ye in me, and I in you.

JOHN 14:16-20, KJV

From Smith Wigglesworth:

The Holy Spirit coming upon an individual changes him and fertilizes his spiritual life. We can reach this place and keep in it—abide in it. Only one thing is going to accomplish the purpose of God—that is to be filled with the Spirit. We must yield and submit, until our bodies are saturated with God—that at any moment God's will can be revealed. We want a great hunger and thirst for God.

Thousands must be brought to the knowledge of the truth. That will only be brought about by human instrumentality, when the instrument is at a place where he will say all the Holy Spirit directs him to. He will dwell in the place of tranquility, where he knows God is controlling, and moves him by the mighty power of His Spirit.

—Abiding in Power

Abide in God and
He will abide in you.

Promises About Abiding

From the Bible:

Abide in me, and I in you. As the branch cannot bear fruit of itself, except it abide in the vine; no more can ye, except ye abide in me.

I am the vine, ye are the branches: He that abideth in me, and I in him, the same bringeth forth much fruit: for without me ye can do nothing.

If a man abide not in me, he is cast forth as a branch, and is withered; and men gather them, and cast them into the fire, and they are burned.

If ye abide in me, and my words abide in you, ye shall ask what ye will, and it shall be done unto you.

If ye keep my commandments, ye shall abide in my love; even as I have kept my Father's commandments, and abide in his love.

These things have I spoken unto you, that my joy might remain in you, and that your joy might be full.

JOHN 15:4-7, 10-11, KJV

From Smith Wigglesworth:

The Bible has so many precious promises, wealth beyond all price. Some people throw over God's wonderful plan for a feeling. Be real, after God's plan. The waverer gets nothing.

Real faith is establishment. How can you get it? Abide under the shadow of the Almighty. Don't change. Have you the presence of God, the glory of God? Pay any price to abide under that covering. The secret of victory is to abide where the victory abides.

—*The Secret Place*

Abide in God and
He will abide in you.

Promises About Abiding

From the Bible:

Let that therefore abide in you, which ye have heard from the beginning. If that which ye have heard from the beginning shall remain in you, ye also shall continue in the Son, and in the Father.

And this is the promise that he hath promised us, even eternal life.

These things have I written unto you concerning them that seduce you.

But the anointing which ye have received of him abideth in you, and ye need not that any man teach you: but as the same anointing teacheth you of all things, and is truth, and is no lie, and even as it hath taught you, ye shall abide in him.

And now, little children, abide in him; that, when he shall appear, we may have confidence, and not be ashamed before him at his coming.

1 JOHN 2:24-28, KJV

From Smith Wigglesworth:

I will say of the Lord, He is my refuge. Who will say it? He that abideth. There is no kick there. No evil temper, no irritability. All is swept away, dwelling in the presence of the Almighty, the covering of God.

Can we keep there?

He never forgets to keep me.

He never forgets to keep me.

My father has many dear children,

But He never forgets to keep me.

Has He forgotten to keep you?

Nay! He cannot forget. God has much in store.

—*The Secret Place*

Abide in God and
He will abide in you.

Promises About Blessing

From the Bible:

The Lord bless you and keep you; the Lord make his face shine upon you and be gracious to you; the Lord turn his face toward you and give you peace.

NUMBERS 6:24-26, NIV

If you pay attention to these laws and are careful to follow them, then the Lord your God will keep his covenant of love with you, as he swore to your forefathers.

He will love you and bless you and increase your numbers. He will bless the fruit of your womb, the crops of your land—your grain, new wine and oil—the calves of your herds and the lambs of your flocks in the land that he swore to your forefathers to give you.

You will be blessed more than any other people.

DEUTERONOMY 7:12-14, NIV

From Smith Wigglesworth:

God bless you! What He blesses, no one can curse. When God is with you it is impossible for anyone to be against you. When God has put His hand upon your way it will open with benediction to others. The greatest thing that God has allowed us is distributing His blessing to others.

Oh, what a blessing to know that we are the fruit of the Lord; His people are the precious fruit of the earth. I am not afraid to say these things because I know God means to bless you. Why should you go away without a blessing when God has promised you a measure that cannot be measured?

—God Bless You!

Follow the Lord's ways
and He will bless you.

Promises About Blessing

From the Bible:

May God be gracious to us and bless us and make his face shine upon us, that your ways may be known on earth, your salvation among all nations.

May the peoples praise you, O God; may all the peoples praise you.

May the nations be glad and sing for joy, for you rule the peoples justly and guide the nations of the earth.

May the peoples praise you, O God; may all the peoples praise you.

Then the land will yield its harvest, and God, our God, will bless us.

God will bless us, and all the ends of the earth will fear him.

PSALM 67, NIV

18

From Smith Wigglesworth:

God has promised to never leave us or forsake us. He promised not to leave Jacob and He did not fail in His promise. He has promised not to leave us and He will not fail.

We need to get alone with God to have a real meeting with Him. He will bring us down. He will change our names. He will transform us from Jacob to Israel. But we need to lay hold of Him.

Jacob held on and clung to Him until the blessing came. If God does not help me I am no good for this world's need. I am no longer salt. It is so easy to lose the savor. But as we get alone with God, He gives us His blessing. He resalts us. He empowers us.

—A Straightened Place
Where God Is Revealed

Follow the Lord's ways
and He will bless you.

Promises About Blessing

From the Bible:

Lead me, O Lord, in your righteousness because of my enemies—make straight your way before me.

But let all who take refuge in you be glad; let them ever sing for joy. Spread your protection over them, that those who love your name may rejoice in you.

For surely, O Lord, you bless the righteous; you surround them with your favor as with a shield.

PSALM 5:8, 11-12, NIV

Praise be to the God and Father of our Lord Jesus Christ, who has blessed us in the heavenly realms with every spiritual blessing in Christ.

EPHESIANS 1:3, NIV

From Smith Wigglesworth:

Abraham attained to the place where he became a friend of God by believing Him. He believed God, and God counted that to him for righteousness. Righteousness was imputed to him on no other ground than that he believed God.

Can this be true of anybody else? Yes, every person in the world who is saved by faith is blessed along with faithful Abraham. The promise came to Abraham because he believed God's promise that in him all the families of the earth should be blessed. When we believe God, there is no knowing where the blessing of our faith will end.

—*Ever Increasing Faith*

Follow the Lord's ways
and He will bless you.

Promises About Calling

From the Bible:

And we know that in all things God works for the good of those who love him, who have been called according to his purpose.

For those God foreknew he also predestined to be conformed to the likeness of his Son, that he might be the firstborn among many brothers.

And those he predestined, he also called; those he called, he also justified; those he justified, he also glorified.

What, then, shall we say in response to this? If God is for us, who can be against us?

He who did not spare his own Son, but gave him up for us all—how will he not also, along with him, graciously give us all things?

Who will bring any charge against those whom God has chosen? It is God who justifies.

ROMANS 8:28-33, NIV

From Smith Wigglesworth:

When a man is born of God, he becomes a quickened soul to carry out the convictions of the Spirit of God in him. When he is born of God, on the threshold of this new birth there comes a vision of what his life is to be.

The question is whether you dare to go through with it, whether you are going to hold on to the very thing the Holy Spirit brought to you. Never lose sight of it, but press on in a life of devotion to God and of fellowship and unity with Him.

—*Our Great Need*

God has called you
for a special purpose.

Promises About Calling

From the Bible:

We preach Christ crucified: a stumbling block to Jews and foolishness to Gentiles, but to those whom God has called, both Jews and Greeks, Christ the power of God and the wisdom of God.

For the foolishness of God is wiser than man's wisdom, and the weakness of God is stronger than man's strength.

Brothers, think of what you were when you were called. Not many of you were wise by human standards; not many were influential; not many were of noble birth.

But God chose the foolish things of the world to shame the wise; God chose the weak things of the world to shame the strong.

He chose the lowly things of this world and the despised things—and the things that are not—to nullify the things that are, so that no one may boast before him.

1 CORINTHIANS 1:23-29, NIV

From Smith Wigglesworth:

Called! Beloved, I know some people who believe that because they have failed in so many things, there is no hope for them in this calling.

Satan comes and says, "Look at the catalog of helpless infirmities! You can never expect to be in the calling!" Yes, you can! God has it in the Scriptures. Weakness is made strong! It is the last that can be first.

What will make the difference? When we confess our helplessness. He says He feeds the hungry with good things, but the satisfied He sends away empty.

—Our Calling

God has called you
for a special purpose.

Promises About Calling

From the Bible:

With this in mind, we constantly pray for you, that our God may count you worthy of his calling, and that by his power he may fulfill every good purpose of yours and every act prompted by your faith.

2 THESSALONIANS 1:11, NIV

Therefore, holy brothers, who share in the heavenly calling, fix your thoughts on Jesus, the apostle and high priest whom we confess.

He was faithful to the one who appointed him, just as Moses was faithful in all God's house.

Jesus has been found worthy of greater honor than Moses, just as the builder of a house has greater honor than the house itself.

For every house is built by someone, but God is the builder of everything.

HEBREWS 3:1-4, NIV

From Smith Wigglesworth:

A man who is baptized with the Holy Spirit has a Jesus mission. He knows his vocation, the plan of his life. God speaks to him so definitely there is no mistaking it.

Thank God for the knowledge which fixes me so solidly upon God's Word that I cannot be moved from it by any storm that may rage. The revelation of Jesus to my soul by the Holy Spirit brings me to a place where I am willing, if need be, to die for what the Word says.

—Our Great Need

God has called you for a special purpose.

Promises About Deliverance

From the Bible:

O Lord, how many are my foes! How many rise up against me!

Many are saying of me, "God will not deliver him."

But you are a shield around me, O Lord; you bestow glory on me and lift up my head.

To the Lord I cry aloud, and he answers me from his holy hill.

I lie down and sleep; I wake again, because the Lord sustains me.

I will not fear the tens of thousands drawn up against me on every side.

Arise, O Lord! Deliver me, O my God! Strike all my enemies on the jaw; break the teeth of the wicked.

From the Lord comes deliverance. May your blessing be on your people.

PSALM 3, NIV

28

From Smith Wigglesworth:

Are you oppressed? Cry out to God. It is always good for people to cry out.

The Holy Spirit and the Word of God will bring to light every hidden, unclean thing that must be revealed. There is a place of deliverance when you let God search out that which is spoiling and marring your life.

Jesus is still the deliverer, exposing the power of evil, delivering the captives and letting the oppressed go free, purifying them and cleansing their hearts.

God is compassionate. See Him now, call on His name right now, and there is forgiveness, healing, redemption, deliverance, and everything you need for now, and that which will satisfy you through eternity.

—*Deliverance to the Captives*

The Lord is your mighty deliverer.

Promises About Deliverance

From the Bible:

Sacrifice thank offerings to God, fulfill your vows to the Most High, and call upon me in the day of trouble; I will deliver you, and you will honor me.

PSALM 50:14-15, NIV

In you, O Lord, I have taken refuge; let me never be put to shame; deliver me in your righteousness.

Turn your ear to me, come quickly to my rescue; be my rock of refuge, a strong fortress to save me.

Since you are my rock and my fortress, for the sake of your name lead and guide me.

Free me from the trap that is set for me, for you are my refuge.

Into your hands I commit my spirit; redeem me, O Lord, the God of truth.

PSALM 31:1-5, NIV

From Smith Wigglesworth:

There is a life of perfect peace, and this is where God wants you to be.

If I find my peace is disturbed, I know it is the enemy who is trying to work. How do I know this? Because the Lord has promised to keep your mind in perfect peace when it is stayed on Him.

As we think about that which is pure, we become pure. As we think about that which is holy, we become holy. And as we think about our Lord Jesus Christ, we become like Him. We are changed into the likeness of the object on which our gaze is fixed.

—The Discerning of Spirits

The Lord is your mighty deliverer.

Promises About Deliverance

From the Bible:

He who dwells in the shelter of the Most High will rest in the shadow of the Almighty.

I will say of the Lord, "He is my refuge and my fortress, my God, in whom I trust."

Surely he will save you from the fowler's snare and from the deadly pestilence.

He will cover you with his feathers, and under his wings you will find refuge; his faithfulness will be your shield and rampart.

"Because he loves me," says the Lord, "I will rescue him; I will protect him, for he acknowledges my name.

"He will call upon me, and I will answer him; I will be with him in trouble, I will deliver him and honor him."

PSALM 91:1-4, 14-15, NIV

From Smith Wigglesworth:

If you are definite with God, you will never go away disappointed. The divine life will flow into you, and you will be delivered.

He has an overflowing cup for you, a fullness of life. He will meet you in your absolute helplessness. All things are possible if you only believe.

God has a real plan. It is so simple.

Just come to Jesus. You will find Him just the same as He was in the days of old.

—Himself Took Our Infirmities

The Lord is your mighty deliverer.

Promises About Deliverance

From the Bible:

May my cry come before you, O Lord; give me understanding according to your word.

May my supplication come before you; deliver me according to your promise.

PSALM 119:169-170, NIV

Forgive us our debts, as we also have forgiven our debtors.

And lead us not into temptation, but deliver us from the evil one.

MATTHEW 6:12-13, NIV

From Smith Wigglesworth:

There are evil powers, but Jesus is greater than all of them. There are tremendous diseases, but Jesus is the healer. There is no case too hard for Him.

The Lion of Judah can break every chain. He came to relieve the oppressed and to set the captives free. He came to bring redemption, to make us as perfect as man was before the Fall.

Every position of grace into which you are led—forgiveness, healing, deliverance of any kind—will be contested by Satan. He will contend for your body. When you are saved, Satan will say, "See, you are not saved." The devil is a liar. If he says you are not saved, it is a sure sign that you are.

—*I Am the Lord That Healeth Thee*

The Lord is your mighty deliverer.

Promises About Faith

From the Bible:

Don't you believe that I am in the Father, and that the Father is in me? The words I say to you are not just my own. Rather, it is the Father, living in me, who is doing his work.

Believe me when I say that I am in the Father and the Father is in me; or at least believe on the evidence of the miracles themselves.

I tell you the truth, anyone who has faith in me will do what I have been doing. He will do even greater things than these, because I am going to the Father.

And I will do whatever you ask in my name, so that the Son may bring glory to the Father.

You may ask me for anything in my name, and I will do it.

JOHN 14:10-14, NIV

From Smith Wigglesworth:

You ask, "What is faith?" Faith is the principle of the Word of God. The Holy Spirit, who inspired the Word, is called the Spirit of Truth.

As we receive with meekness the engrafted Word, faith springs up in our hearts—faith in the sacrifice of Calvary; faith in the shed blood of Jesus; faith in the fact that He took our weaknesses upon Himself, has borne our sicknesses and carried our pains, and that He is our life today.

—I Am the Lord That Healeth Thee

Faith in God
accomplishes great things.

Promises About Faith

From the Bible:

As Jesus went on from there, two blind men followed him, calling out, "Have mercy on us, Son of David!"

When he had gone indoors, the blind men came to him, and he asked them, "Do you believe that I am able to do this?" "Yes, Lord," they replied.

Then he touched their eyes and said, "According to your faith will it be done to you."

MATTHEW 9:27-29, NIV

The apostles said to the Lord, "Increase our faith!"

He replied, "If you have faith as small as a mustard seed, you can say to this mulberry tree, 'Be uprooted and planted in the sea,' and it will obey you."

LUKE 17:5-6, NIV

From Smith Wigglesworth:

The greatest weakness in the world is unbelief. The greatest power is the faith that worketh by love. Love, mercy, and grace are bound eternally to faith.

Fear is the opposite of faith, but there is no fear in love, and those whose hearts are filled with a divine faith and love have no question in their hearts about being caught up when Jesus comes.

The world is filled with fear, torment, remorse, and brokenness, but faith and love are sure to overcome.

—*The Way to Overcome: Believe!*

Faith in God
accomplishes great things.

Promises About Faith

From the Bible:

For in the gospel a righteousness from God is revealed, a righteousness that is by faith from first to last, just as it is written: "The righteous will live by faith."

Therefore, the promise comes by faith, so that it may be by grace and may be guaranteed to all of Abraham's offspring—not only to those who are of the law but also to those who are of the faith of Abraham.

ROMANS 1:17; 4:16, NIV

Consequently, faith comes from hearing the message, and the message is heard through the word of Christ.

ROMANS 10:17, NIV

From Smith Wigglesworth:

Oh, this wonderful faith of the Lord Jesus. Our faith comes to an end. How many times I have been to the place where I told the Lord, "I have used all the faith I have," and then He has placed His own faith within me.

One of our workers said to me, "I never was so near the end of my purse in my life."

I replied, "Thank God, you are just at the opening of God's treasures."

It is when we are at the end of our own that we can enter into the riches of God's resources. It is when we possess nothing that we can possess all things.

The Lord will always meet you when you have living faith.

—The Word of Knowledge and Faith

Faith in God accomplishes great things.

Promises About Faith

From the Bible:

Now faith is being sure of what we hope for and certain of what we do not see.

By faith we understand that the universe was formed at God's command, so that what is seen was not made out of what was visible.

And without faith it is impossible to please God, because anyone who comes to him must believe that he exists and that he rewards those who earnestly seek him.

HEBREWS 11:1, 3, 6, NIV

From Smith Wigglesworth:

Faith is the substance of things hoped for.

Someone said to me one day, "I would not believe in anything I could not handle and see." Everything you handle and see is temporary and will perish with the using. But the things not seen are eternal and will not fade away.

Are you dealing with tangible things or eternal things, the things that are facts or the things that are made real to faith?

Thank God that through the Son of God I have within me a greater power, a mightier working, an inward impact of life, of power, of vision, and of truth more real than anyone who lives in the realm of the tangible.

God manifests Himself to the person who dares to believe.

—*The Substance of Things Hoped For*

Faith in God
accomplishes great things.

Promises About Faith

From the Bible:

Was not our ancestor Abraham considered righteous for what he did when he offered his son Isaac on the altar?

You see that his faith and his actions were working together, and his faith was made complete by what he did.

And the scripture was fulfilled that says, "Abraham believed God, and it was credited to him as righteousness," and he was called God's friend.

You see that a person is justified by what he does and not by faith alone.

As the body without the spirit is dead, so faith without deeds is dead.

JAMES 2:21-24, 26, NIV

From Smith Wigglesworth:

Faith is a reality, and God wants to bring us to the fact of it. He wants us to know that we have something greater than we can see or handle, because everything we can see and handle is going to pass away.

The Lord has a way of making you able to live in power as long as you have learned the lesson needed. God will make us know how to live.

When you are in the right attitude, faith becomes remarkably active. But it can never be remarkably active in a dead life. It is when sin is out and the body is clean and the life is made right that the Holy Spirit comes, and faith brings the evidence.

—Dominant Faith

Faith in God
accomplishes great things.

Promises About Freedom

From the Bible:

I will walk about in freedom, for I have sought out your precepts.

I will speak of your statutes before kings and will not be put to shame, for I delight in your commands because I love them.

Psalm 119:45-47, NIV

[Jesus said,] "Then you will know the truth, and the truth will set you free."

They answered him, "We are Abraham's descendants and have never been slaves of anyone. How can you say that we shall be set free?"

Jesus replied, "I tell you the truth, everyone who sins is a slave to sin.

"Now a slave has no permanent place in the family, but a son belongs to it forever.

"So if the Son sets you free, you will be free indeed."

JOHN 8:32-36, NIV

From Smith Wigglesworth:

Remember that God has so wonderfully overcome the power of Satan and the powers of disease and the powers of sin till there is a perfect place in Christ Jesus, where we may be free from sin, sickness, disease, and death. It is one of the greatest positions that God has for us.

If I were to select a word to meet your need, you would find it in Romans 8:1-2: "There is therefore now no condemnation to them which are in Christ Jesus, who walk not after the flesh, but after the Spirit. For the law of the Spirit of life in Christ Jesus has made me free from the law of sin and death."

—Faith and Prayer

Christ sets you free
from what binds you.

Promises About Freedom

From the Bible:

[Jesus read,] "The Spirit of the Lord is on me, because he has anointed me to preach good news to the poor. He has sent me to proclaim freedom for the prisoners and recovery of sight for the blind, to release the oppressed, to proclaim the year of the Lord's favor."

LUKE 4:18-19, NIV

The creation waits in eager expectation for the sons of God to be revealed.

For the creation was subjected to frustration, not by its own choice, but by the will of the one who subjected it, in hope that the creation itself will be liberated from its bondage to decay and brought into the glorious freedom of the children of God.

ROMANS 8:19-21, NIV

Now the Lord is the Spirit, and where the Spirit of the Lord is, there is freedom.

2 CORINTHIANS 3:17, NIV

From Smith Wigglesworth:

Only believe!
Only believe!
All things are possible,
Only believe!

Praise God, He has made all things possible. There is liberty for everyone, whatever the trouble. He has obtained freedom from every difficulty, over every power of evil, over every depravity. Every sin is covered by Calvary.

—*Full! Full! Full!*

Christ sets you free
from what binds you.

Promises About Freedom

From the Bible:

You, my brothers, were called to be free. But do not use your freedom to indulge the sinful nature; rather, serve one another in love.

GALATIANS 5:13, NIV

In him and through faith in him we may approach God with freedom and confidence.

EPHESIANS 3:12, NIV

Live as free men, but do not use your freedom as a cover-up for evil; live as servants of God.

1 Peter 2:16, NIV

From Smith Wigglesworth:

If the Word of God is in your heart you will be free. God is always making you free. The gospel is full of liberty, and no bondage. *Full of liberty.*

How long does it take to get clean? Jesus said, "I will, be thou clean," and immediately a man's leprosy was cleansed.

Lots of people have a great block in their way. They say, "I wonder if it is God's will" and then give up.

Is it the will of God? It falls in line with redemption. To all who believe, God's plan is clear. The plan is "I will when you will."

—*The Deliverance of Multitudes*

Christ sets you free
from what binds you.

Promises About God

From the Bible:

I will walk among you and be your God, and you will be my people.

LEVITICUS 26:12, NIV

And now, O Israel, what does the Lord your God ask of you but to fear the Lord your God, to walk in all his ways, to love him, to serve the Lord your God with all your heart and with all your soul.

DEUTERONOMY 10:12, NIV

From Smith Wigglesworth:

Wanting God! Wanting the fellowship of the Spirit! Wanting the walk with Him! Wanting communion with Him! Everything else is no good.

You want the association with God, and God says, "I will come and walk with you. I will sup with you and you with Me, and I will live in you."

A joyful hallelujah! We can attain to a spiritual majority, a fullness of Christ, a place where God becomes the perfect Father and the Holy Spirit has a rightful place as never before.

The Holy Spirit breathes through us and says, "You are my Father, You are my Father." The Spirit cries, "Abba Father, My Father." Oh, it is wonderful! And may God grant to us the richness of His pleasure, that unfolding of His will, that consciousness of His countenance upon us.

—Sonship

Nothing can separate you from God's love.

Promises About God

From the Bible:

Very rarely will anyone die for a righteous man, though for a good man someone might possibly dare to die.

But God demonstrates his own love for us in this: While we were still sinners, Christ died for us.

ROMANS 5:7-8, NIV

In all these things we are more than conquerors through him who loved us.

For I am convinced that neither death nor life, neither angels nor demons, neither the present nor the future, nor any powers, neither height nor depth, nor anything else in all creation, will be able to separate us from the love of God that is in Christ Jesus our Lord.

ROMANS 8:37-39, NIV

From Smith Wigglesworth:

It is impossible to comprehend the love of God as we think on natural lines. We must have the revelation from the Spirit of God. God gives liberally. He who asks, receives.

God is willing to bestow on us all things that pertain to life and godliness. Oh, it was the love of God that brought Jesus. And it is this same love that helps you and me to believe.

In every weakness God will be your strength. You who need His touch, remember that He loves you.

—Have Faith in God

Nothing can separate you
from God's love.

Promises About God

From the Bible:

Or do you show contempt for the riches of his kindness, tolerance and patience, not realizing that God's kindness leads you toward repentance?

But what if some did not have faith? Will their lack of faith nullify God's faithfulness? Not at all!

ROMANS 2:4; 3:3-4a, NIV

Consider therefore the kindness and sternness of God: sternness to those who fell, but kindness to you, provided that you continue in his kindness.

ROMANS 11:22, NIV

From Smith Wigglesworth:

As Paul saw the depths and heights of the grandeur of God, he longed that he might win Him. Before his conversion, in his passion and zeal, Paul would do anything to bring Christians to death. That passion raged like a mighty lion. As he was going to Damascus, he heard the voice of Jesus saying, "Saul, Saul, why persecutest thou me?" What broke him was the tenderness of God.

Beloved, it is always God's tenderness over our weakness and depravity that breaks us as well. If somebody came along to thwart us, we would stand our ground, but when we come to the one who forgives us, we are overwhelmed.

Oh, to win Him!

—*The Anointing of His Spirit*

Nothing can separate you
from God's love.

Promises About God

From the Bible:

May our Lord Jesus Christ himself and God our Father, who loved us and by his grace gave us eternal encouragement and good hope, encourage your hearts and strengthen you in every good deed and word.

2 THESSALONIANS 2:16-17, NIV

There remains, then, a Sabbath-rest for the people of God; for anyone who enters God's rest also rests from his own work, just as God did from his.

Let us, therefore, make every effort to enter that rest, so that no one will fall by following their example of disobedience.

HEBREWS 4:9-11, NIV

From Smith Wigglesworth:

Oh, we need to get alone with God, we need to be broken, we need to be changed, we need to be transformed. When we meet with God, when He interposes, all care and strife comes to an end. Get alone with God and receive the revelation of His infinite grace and wonderful purposes and plans for your life.

The person baptized in the Holy Spirit keeps in touch with his Master, wherever he may be. He has no room for anything that steps lower than the unction that was on his Master, or for anything that hinders him from being about his Master's business.

—Only Believe!

Nothing can separate you
from God's love.

Promises About God's Word

From the Bible:

I seek you with all my heart; do not let me stray from your commands.

I have hidden your word in my heart that I might not sin against you.

Praise be to you, O Lord; teach me your decrees.

With my lips I recount all the laws that come from your mouth.

I rejoice in following your statutes as one rejoices in great riches.

I meditate on your precepts and consider your ways.

I delight in your decrees; I will not neglect your word.

Do good to your servant, and I will live; I will obey your word.

PSALM 119:10-17, NIV

From Smith Wigglesworth:

The psalmist said that he hid God's Word in his heart, that he might not sin against Him. You will find that the more of God's Word you hide in your heart, the easier it is to live a holy life.

He also testified that God's Word had quickened him. As you receive God's Word into your being, you will be quickened and made strong.

As you receive with meekness the Word, you will find faith springing up within. You will have life through the Word.

—*What It Means to Be Full of the Holy Spirit*

God's Word is a light for your path.

Promises About God's Word

From the Bible:

Your word is a lamp to my feet and a light for my path.

Psalm 119:105, niv

The grass withers and the flowers fall, but the word of our God stands forever.

Isaiah 40:8, niv

As the rain and the snow come down from heaven, and do not return to it without watering the earth and making it bud and flourish, so that it yields seed for the sower and bread for the eater, so is my word that goes out from my mouth: It will not return to me empty, but will accomplish what I desire and achieve the purpose for which I sent it.

Isaiah 55:10-11, niv

From Smith Wigglesworth:

There are thousands of people who read and study the Word of God. But it is not quickened to them. The Bible is a dead letter except by the Spirit. The Word of God can never be vital and powerful in us except by the Spirit. The words that Christ spoke are spirit and life.

It is a blessed thing to learn that God's Word can never fail. Never hearken to human plans. God can work mightily when you persist in believing Him in spite of discouragements from the human standpoint.

—The Power of the Name

God's Word is a light for your path.

Promises About God's Word

From the Bible:

This is the one I esteem: he who is humble and contrite in spirit, and trembles at my word.

ISAIAH 66:2, NIV

Jesus answered, "It is written: 'Man does not live on bread alone, but on every word that comes from the mouth of God.'"

MATTHEW 4:4, NIV

The Word became flesh and made his dwelling among us. We have seen his glory, the glory of the One and Only, who came from the Father, full of grace and truth.

JOHN 1:14, NIV

From Smith Wigglesworth:

I know that God's Word is sufficient. One word from Him can change a nation. His Word is from everlasting to everlasting.

It is through the entrance of this everlasting Word, this incorruptible seed, that we are born again and come into this wonderful salvation.

Man cannot live by bread alone, but must live by every word that proceedeth out of the mouth of God. This is the food of faith. Faith cometh by hearing and hearing by the Word of God.

—Have Faith in God

God's Word is a light for your path.

Promises About God's Word

From the Bible:

Let the word of Christ dwell in you richly as you
teach and admonish one another with all wisdom,
and as you sing psalms, hymns and spiritual songs
with gratitude in your hearts to God.

COLOSSIANS 3:16, NIV

And we also thank God continually because, when
you received the word of God, which you heard
from us, you accepted it not as the word of men,
but as it actually is, the word of God, which is at
work in you who believe.

1 THESSALONIANS 2:13, NIV

All Scripture is God-breathed and is useful for
teaching, rebuking, correcting and training in
righteousness, so that the man of God may be
thoroughly equipped for every good work.

2 TIMOTHY 3:16-17, NIV

From Smith Wigglesworth:

You have to believe the Word of God and not change it because of people who have other opinions. Take the Word of God. It will furnish you in every good stand.

It is there you will find out you want nothing better; there is nothing better. It is there you will find all you want: food for hunger, light for darkness, largeness of heart, conception of thought, inspiration for life.

—*God Bless You!*

God's Word is a light for your path.

Promises About God's Word

From the Bible:

For the word of God is living and active. Sharper than any double-edged sword, it penetrates even to dividing soul and spirit, joints and marrow; it judges the thoughts and attitudes of the heart.

HEBREWS 4:12, NIV

Do not merely listen to the word, and so deceive yourselves. Do what it says.

Anyone who listens to the word but does not do what it says is like a man who looks at his face in a mirror and, after looking at himself, goes away and immediately forgets what he looks like.

But the man who looks intently into the perfect law that gives freedom, and continues to do this, not forgetting what he has heard, but doing it — he will be blessed in what he does.

JAMES 1:22-25, NIV

From Smith Wigglesworth:

The child of God ought to thirst for the Word. He should know the Word, and know nothing among men save Jesus.

It is as we feed on the Word and meditate on its message that the Spirit of God can vitalize what we have received and bring forth through us the word of knowledge. It will be as full of power and life as when the Spirit of God moved upon holy men of old and gave them inspired Scriptures. They were all inspired of God, and through the same Spirit words can come forth from us vitalized, living, powerful, and sharper than a two-edged sword.

—*The Word of Knowledge and Faith*

God's Word is a light for your path.

Promises About Healing

From the Bible:

He said, "If you listen carefully to the voice of the Lord your God and do what is right in his eyes, if you pay attention to his commands and keep all his decrees, I will not bring on you any of the diseases I brought on the Egyptians, for I am the Lord, who heals you."

EXODUS 15:26, NIV

Praise the Lord, O my soul, and forget not all his benefits—who forgives all your sins and heals all your diseases.

PSALM 103:2-3, NIV

He heals the brokenhearted and binds up their wounds.

PSALM 147:3, NIV

From Smith Wigglesworth:

You will find that those who are healed by the power of God—especially believers—will find their healing an incentive to make them purer and holier. If divine healing was merely to make the body whole, it would be worth very little.

Divine healing is the providence of God coming into your mortal bodies, and after being touched by Almightiness, can you remain the same? No.

Like me, you will worship and serve God.

—*The Incarnation of Man*

The Lord heals
both body and soul.

Promises About Healing

From the Bible:

He was despised and rejected by men, a man of sorrows, and familiar with suffering. Like one from whom men hide their faces he was despised, and we esteemed him not.

Surely he took up our infirmities and carried our sorrows, yet we considered him stricken by God, smitten by him, and afflicted.

But he was pierced for our transgressions, he was crushed for our iniquities; the punishment that brought us peace was upon him, and by his wounds we are healed.

We all, like sheep, have gone astray, each of us has turned to his own way; and the Lord has laid on him the iniquity of us all.

ISAIAH 53:3-6, NIV

From Smith Wigglesworth:

Look to God. Only believe that His atoning blood is sufficient and you will be healed from weakness.

The God who told Moses to make a pole and put a brazen serpent upon it, that whoever looked could be healed, now says the brazen serpent is no longer on the pole. Jesus is no longer on the cross, so now believe, and you shall be healed if you believe.

You cannot look to the cross, you cannot look to the serpent, but you can believe, and if you believe, you will be healed. God means for you to look to Him today. God means for you to be helped today.

—*The Place of Reigning*

The Lord heals
both body and soul.

Promises About Healing

From the Bible:

"I have seen his ways, but I will heal him; I will guide him and restore comfort to him, creating praise on the lips of the mourners in Israel. Peace, peace, to those far and near," says the Lord. "And I will heal them."

ISAIAH 57:18-19, NIV

"I will heal my people and will let them enjoy abundant peace and security."

JEREMIAH 33:6, NIV

But for you who revere my name, the sun of righteousness will rise with healing in its wings. And you will go out and leap like calves released from the stall.

MALACHI 4:2, NIV

74

From Smith Wigglesworth:

Jesus rebuked sickness and it went, and I want you to see that you can be healed.

You must give God your life; then sickness can go and God can come in. Your lives have to be clean, and God can keep you holy. You have to walk before God, and He can make you perfect.

For God says without holiness no man shall see Him. As we walk in the light as He is in the light, we have fellowship with one another, and the blood of Jesus Christ, God's Son, cleanses us from all sin.

—Divine Life and Divine Health

The Lord heals both body and soul.

Promises About Healing

From the Bible:

For this people's heart has become calloused; they hardly hear with their ears, and they have closed their eyes. Otherwise they might see with their eyes, hear with their ears, understand with their hearts and turn, and I would heal them.

But blessed are your eyes because they see, and your ears because they hear.

MATTHEW 13:15-16, NIV

When Jesus had called the Twelve together, he gave them power and authority to drive out all demons and to cure diseases, and he sent them out to preach the kingdom of God and to heal the sick.

LUKE 9:1-2, NIV

From Smith Wigglesworth:

The Word can drive disease from our bodies. It is our portion in Christ—Him who is our bread, our life, our health, our all in all. And though we may be deep in sin, we can come to Him in repentance and He will forgive, cleanse, and heal us.

His words are spirit and life to those who will receive them. The life of Jesus Christ, God's Son, can so purify our hearts and minds that we become transformed in spirit, soul, and body.

—Ever Increasing Faith

The Lord heals
both body and soul.

Promises About Healing

From the Bible:

Is any one of you sick? He should call the elders of the church to pray over him and anoint him with oil in the name of the Lord.

And the prayer offered in faith will make the sick person well; the Lord will raise him up. If he has sinned, he will be forgiven.

Therefore confess your sins to each other and pray for each other so that you may be healed. The prayer of a righteous man is powerful and effective.

Elijah was a man just like us. He prayed earnestly that it would not rain, and it did not rain on the land for three and a half years.

Again he prayed, and the heavens gave rain, and the earth produced its crops.

JAMES 5:14-18, NIV

From Smith Wigglesworth:

We have in this precious Word a real basis for the truth of healing. In this Scripture God gives very definite instructions to the sick.

If you are sick, your part is to call for the elders of the church. It is their part to anoint and pray for you in faith, and then the situation rests with the Lord.

When you have been anointed and prayed for, you can rest assured that the Lord can raise you up. It is the Word of God.

—*Wilt Thou Be Made Whole?*

The Lord heals
both body and soul.

Promises About the Holy Spirit

From the Bible:

[John the Baptist said,] "I baptize you with water for repentance. But after me will come one who is more powerful than I, whose sandals I am not fit to carry. He will baptize you with the Holy Spirit and with fire."

MATTHEW 3:11, NIV

[Jesus said,] "Therefore go and make disciples of all nations, baptizing them in the name of the Father and of the Son and of the Holy Spirit, and teaching them to obey everything I have commanded you. And surely I am with you always, to the very end of the age."

MATTHEW 28:19-20, NIV

From Smith Wigglesworth:

It is impossible to overestimate the importance of being filled with the Spirit. It is impossible for us to meet the conditions of the day—to walk in the light as He is in the light, to subdue kingdoms, to work righteousness, and to bind the power of Satan—unless we are filled with the Holy Spirit.

Yes, there is a power, a blessing, an assurance, a rest in the presence of the Holy Spirit. You can feel His presence and know that He is with you. You need not spend an hour without this inner knowledge of His holy presence.

—*Concerning Spiritual Gifts*

You can be filled
with the Spirit's fire.

Promises About the Holy Spirit

From the Bible:

"So I say to you: Ask and it will be given to you; seek and you will find; knock and the door will be opened to you.

"For everyone who asks receives; he who seeks finds; and to him who knocks, the door will be opened.

"Which of you fathers, if your son asks for a fish, will give him a snake instead?

"Or if he asks for an egg, will give him a scorpion?

"If you then, though you are evil, know how to give good gifts to your children, how much more will your Father in heaven give the Holy Spirit to those who ask him!"

LUKE 11:9-13, NIV

From Smith Wigglesworth:

There is more for us all yet, praise the Lord! This is only the beginning. So far we have only touched the fringe of things. There is so much more for us if we will yield to God.

Do you want to receive the Spirit? Jesus said, "If ye, being evil, know how to give good gifts to your children, how much more shall your heavenly Father give the Holy Spirit to them that ask him?"

I am a father and I want to give my boys the very best. We human fathers are but finite, but our heavenly Father is infinite. There is no limit to the power and blessing He has laid up for them that love Him.

Be filled with the Spirit.

—*Ye Shall Receive Power*

You can be filled with the Spirit's fire.

Promises About the Holy Spirit

From the Bible:

Jesus replied, "If anyone loves me, he will obey my teaching. My Father will love him, and we will come to him and make our home with him.

"He who does not love me will not obey my teaching. These words you hear are not my own; they belong to the Father who sent me.

"All this I have spoken while still with you.

"But the Counselor, the Holy Spirit, whom the Father will send in my name, will teach you all things and will remind you of everything I have said to you.

"Peace I leave with you; my peace I give you. I do not give to you as the world gives. Do not let your hearts be troubled and do not be afraid."

JOHN 14:23-27, NIV

From Smith Wigglesworth:

I don't know a word that could be so fitting at this time as the word *Comforter.*

Jesus ascended. When He ascended, He prayed to the Father that He would send the Comforter. A needy moment; a needy hour; a necessity. Why? Because the disciples would want comforting.

How can they be comforted? By taking the word of Christ and revealing it unto them. What could help them so much as a word by the Spirit? The Spirit is breath, is life, is Person, is power. The breath of Himself to us, the nature of Him.

When you receive the Holy Spirit, you receive the Spirit of Truth, the Spirit of Revelation, the Spirit that takes the words of Jesus and makes them life to you. In the needy moment He is the Comforter.

—*The Baptism of the Holy Spirit*

You can be filled with the Spirit's fire.

Promises About the Holy Spirit

From the Bible:

"For John baptized with water, but in a few days you will be baptized with the Holy Spirit."

ACTS 1:5, NIV

May the God of hope fill you with all joy and peace as you trust in him, so that you may overflow with hope by the power of the Holy Spirit.

ROMANS 15:13, NIV

Do you not know that your body is a temple of the Holy Spirit, who is in you, whom you have received from God? You are not your own; you were bought at a price. Therefore honor God with your body.

1 CORINTHIANS 6:19-20, NIV

From Smith Wigglesworth:

Halt! Think! What is the attitude of your life?

Are you thirsty? Are you longing? Are you willing to pay the price? Are you willing to forfeit in order to have? Are you willing to die that you may live?

Are you willing for Him to have the right-of-way to your heart, your conscience, and all you are? Are you ready to have God's deluge of blessing upon your soul?

Are you ready? You say, for what? That you may be changed forever. Receive the Holy Spirit and be filled with divine power forever.

—*Untitled Bible Study*

You can be filled with the Spirit's fire.

Promises About the Holy Spirit

From the Bible:

Be very careful, then, how you live—not as unwise but as wise, making the most of every opportunity, because the days are evil.

Therefore do not be foolish, but understand what the Lord's will is.

Do not get drunk on wine, which leads to debauchery. Instead, be filled with the Spirit.

Speak to one another with psalms, hymns and spiritual songs. Sing and make music in your heart to the Lord, always giving thanks to God the Father for everything, in the name of our Lord Jesus Christ.

EPHESIANS 5:15-20, NIV

From Smith Wigglesworth:

But I must recognize the difference between my own spirit and the Holy Spirit. My own spirit can do certain things, can even weep and pray and worship, but it is all on a human plane. We must not depend on our human thoughts and activities or on our personality.

If the baptism of the Holy Spirit means anything to you, it brings you to the death of the ordinary, when you are no longer putting faith in your own understanding. But, conscious of your own poverty, you yield to the Spirit. There your body becomes filled with heaven on earth.

—*Present-Time Blessings for Present-Time Saints*

You can be filled with the Spirit's fire.

Promises About Inheritance

From the Bible:

And you also were included in Christ when you heard the word of truth, the gospel of your salvation. Having believed, you were marked in him with a seal, the promised Holy Spirit, who is a deposit guaranteeing our inheritance until the redemption of those who are God's possession— to the praise of his glory.

For this reason, ever since I heard about your faith in the Lord Jesus and your love for all the saints, I have not stopped giving thanks for you, remembering you in my prayers.

I keep asking that the God of our Lord Jesus Christ, the glorious Father, may give you the Spirit of wisdom and revelation, so that you may know him better.

I pray also that the eyes of your heart may be enlightened in order that you may know the hope to which he has called you, the riches of his glorious inheritance in the saints, and his incomparably great power for us who believe.

EPHESIANS 1:13-19, NIV

From Smith Wigglesworth:

I believe the Lord wants us to know our inheritance.

You know there is such a thing as having something left to you. For instance, many people make wills and they leave executors to carry them out. There is one will that has been left, and He who made it is our Lord Jesus Christ. After He was dead He rose to carry out His own will. And now we may have all left to us by Him: all the inheritances, all the blessings, all the power, all the life, all the victory.

All the promises are ours because He is risen.

—*Our Inheritance*

You are an heir to God's great kingdom.

Promises About Inheritance

From the Bible:

And we pray this in order that you may live a life worthy of the Lord and may please him in every way: bearing fruit in every good work, growing in the knowledge of God, being strengthened with all power according to his glorious might so that you may have great endurance and patience, and joyfully giving thanks to the Father, who has qualified you to share in the inheritance of the saints in the kingdom of light.

For he has rescued us from the dominion of darkness and brought us into the kingdom of the Son he loves, in whom we have redemption, the forgiveness of sins.

COLOSSIANS 1:10-14, NIV

From Smith Wigglesworth:

God has shown us the power of sonship. Sons of God may speak and it is done. They may bind things that are loose, and loose things that are bound.

Beloved, in our finite condition it's impossible to estimate the loving kindness of God or the measureless mind of God.

When we come into like-mindedness with God, we begin to see the inheritance God has for us in the Word. This is an exhaustless subject, but I pray God will make you an exhaustless people.

—Sonship

You are an heir to
God's great kingdom.

Promises About Inheritance

From the Bible:

How great is the love the Father has lavished on us, that we should be called children of God! And that is what we are! The reason the world does not know us is that it did not know him.

Dear friends, now we are children of God, and what we will be has not yet been made known. But we know that when he appears, we shall be like him, for we shall see him as he is.

Everyone who has this hope in him purifies himself, just as he is pure.

1 JOHN 3:1-3, NIV

From Smith Wigglesworth:

The Spirit brings us to a place where we understand that we are sons of God. And because of this glorious position we are not only sons but heirs, and not only heirs, but joint heirs with Christ. Because of that, all the promises of God are yea and amen to you through Jesus, in the Holy Spirit.

If the Spirit of God who raised Jesus from the dead is in you, that power of the Spirit will quicken your mortal body. It brings you into a living place to believe that, as an adopted child, you may lay hold of the promises.

I see two wonderful things: I see deliverance for the body, and I see the power of the Spirit in sonship raising us up and pressing us onward through faith in the Lord Jesus Christ.

—Sons and Joint Heirs

You are an heir to
God's great kingdom.

Promises About Jesus Christ

From the Bible:

Now this is eternal life: that they may know you, the only true God, and Jesus Christ, whom you have sent.

JOHN 17:3, NIV

This righteousness from God comes through faith in Jesus Christ to all who believe. There is no difference, for all have sinned and fall short of the glory of God, and are justified freely by his grace through the redemption that came by Christ Jesus.

God presented him as a sacrifice of atonement, through faith in his blood.

ROMANS 3:22-25A, NIV

From Smith Wigglesworth:

Jesus is a wonderful lover! I have been wayward, I have been stubborn. I had an unmanageable temper at one time, but how patient He has been. I am here to tell you that there is power in Jesus and in His wondrous name to transform anyone, to heal anyone.

If only you will see Him as God's Lamb, as God's beloved Son who took the iniquity of us all. If only you will see that Jesus paid the whole price for our redemption that we might be free, you can enter into your purchased inheritance of salvation, life, and power.

—The Power of the Name

Jesus paid the price for all your sins.

Promises About Jesus Christ

From the Bible:

For if, by the trespass of the one man, death reigned through that one man, how much more will those who receive God's abundant provision of grace and of the gift of righteousness reign in life through the one man, Jesus Christ.

Consequently, just as the result of one trespass was condemnation for all men, so also the result of one act of righteousness was justification that brings life for all men.

For just as through the disobedience of the one man the many were made sinners, so also through the obedience of the one man the many will be made righteous.

The law was added so that the trespass might increase. But where sin increased, grace increased all the more, so that, just as sin reigned in death, so also grace might reign through righteousness to bring eternal life through Jesus Christ our Lord.

ROMANS 5:17-21, NIV

From Smith Wigglesworth:

Our Christ is risen. He is a living Christ who indwells us. We must not have this truth merely as a theory. Christ must be risen in us by the power of the Spirit.

The power that raised Him from the dead can animate us, and as this glorious resurrection power surges through us, we will be freed from our weaknesses and we will become strong in the Lord and in the power of His might.

There is a resurrection power that God wants us to have today.

Why not? Receive your portion here and now.

—Our Risen Christ

Jesus paid the price for all your sins.

Promises About Jesus Christ

From the Bible:

Thanks be to God—through Jesus Christ our Lord! So then, I myself in my mind am a slave to God's law, but in the sinful nature a slave to the law of sin.

Therefore, there is now no condemnation for those who are in Christ Jesus, because through Christ Jesus the law of the Spirit of life set me free from the law of sin and death.

For what the law was powerless to do in that it was weakened by the sinful nature, God did by sending his own Son in the likeness of sinful man to be a sin offering. And so he condemned sin in sinful man, in order that the righteous requirements of the law might be fully met in us, who do not live according to the sinful nature but according to the Spirit.

ROMANS 7:25–8:4, NIV

From Smith Wigglesworth:

All things are possible through the name of Jesus. God has highly exalted Him, and given Him the name which is above every name, that at the name of Jesus every knee should bow.

There is power to overcome everything in the world through the name of Jesus. I am looking forward to a wonderful union through the name of Jesus. There is no other name under heaven given among men whereby we must be saved.

—*The Power of the Name*

Jesus paid the price for all your sins.

Promises About Jesus Christ

From the Bible:

But you were washed, you were sanctified, you were justified in the name of the Lord Jesus Christ and by the Spirit of our God.

1 CORINTHIANS 6:11, NIV

There is but one God, the Father, from whom all things came and for whom we live; and there is but one Lord, Jesus Christ, through whom all things came and through whom we live.

1 CORINTHIANS 8:6, NIV

For you know the grace of our Lord Jesus Christ, that though he was rich, yet for your sakes he became poor, so that you through his poverty might become rich.

2 CORINTHIANS 8:9, NIV

From Smith Wigglesworth:

I want to show you how rich you may be, that in everything you can be enriched in Christ Jesus. He has an abundance of grace and the gift of righteousness, and through His abundant grace all things are possible.

You can be a living branch of the living vine, Christ Jesus, and it is your privilege to be what He is. John tells us, "As He is, so are we in this world." Not that we are anything in ourselves, but Christ within us is our all in all.

The Lord Jesus is always wanting to show forth His grace and love in order to draw us to Himself. He is willing to manifest His Word and to let us know the mind of our God.

—*Himself Took Our Infirmities*
and Bare Our Sickness

Jesus paid the price for all your sins.

Promises About Jesus Christ

From the Bible:

For God did not appoint us to suffer wrath but to receive salvation through our Lord Jesus Christ.

He died for us so that, whether we are awake or asleep, we may live together with him.

1 THESSALONIANS 5:9-10, NIV

Jesus Christ is the same yesterday and today and forever.

Through Jesus, therefore, let us continually offer to God a sacrifice of praise—the fruit of lips that confess his name.

HEBREWS 13:8, 15, NIV

From Smith Wigglesworth:

Oh, this wonderful Jesus of ours! He comes and indwells us. He comes to abide. He it is who baptizes us with the Holy Spirit and makes everything different.

We are to be a kind of firstfruits unto God and are to be like Christ who is the Firstfruit, walking in His footsteps, living in power. What a salvation this is, having this risen Christ in us. Everything else must go to nothingness, helplessness, and ruin.

Even the best thought of holiness must be on the decrease so Christ may increase, and all things are under the power of the Spirit.

—Our Risen Christ

Jesus paid the price for all your sins.

Promises About Miracles

From the Bible:

O give thanks to the Lord, call on his name, make known his deeds among the peoples.

Sing to him, sing praises to him, tell of all his wonderful works.

Glory in his holy name; let the hearts of those who seek the Lord rejoice.

Seek the Lord and his strength, seek his presence continually.

Remember the wonderful works he has done, his miracles, and the judgments he uttered.

1 CHRONICLES 16:8-12, NRSV

From Smith Wigglesworth:

You may be ordinary, but God wants to make you extraordinary in the Holy Spirit. God is ready to touch and transform you right now.

Once a woman stood in a meeting, asking for prayer. I prayed for her and she was healed. She cried out, "It's a miracle! It's a miracle! It's a miracle!"

That is what God wants to do. As soon as we get free in the Holy Spirit, something happens. Let us pursue the best thing and let God have His right of way.

—*The Anointing of the Spirit*

You can trust God for a miracle.

Promises About Miracles

From the Bible:

For he is the living God, enduring forever. His kingdom shall never be destroyed, and his dominion has no end.

He delivers and rescues, he works signs and wonders in heaven and on earth.

DANIEL 6:26-27, NRSV

I will call to mind the deeds of the Lord; I will remember your wonders of old.

I will meditate on all your work, and muse on your mighty deeds.

Your way, O God, is holy. What god is so great as our God?

You are the God who works wonders; you have displayed your might among the peoples.

PSALM 77:11-14, NRSV

From Smith Wigglesworth:

There are boundless possibilities for us if we dare to believe that the wonderful virtue of our living Christ shall be made manifest through us as we lay our hands on the sick in His name.

The exceeding great and precious promises of the Word are given to us that we might be partakers in the divine nature. I feel the Holy Spirit is grieved with us because, when we know these things, we do not do exploits for God.

Does not the Holy Spirit show us wide open doors of opportunity? Shall we not let God take us on to greater things? Shall we not believe God to take us on to greater manifestations of His power?

—*Righteousness*

You can trust God for a miracle.

Promises About Miracles

From the Bible:

There is none like you among the gods, O Lord, nor are there any works like yours.

All the nations you have made shall come and bow down before you, O Lord, and shall glorify your name.

For you are great and do wondrous things; you alone are God.

PSALM 86:8-10, NRSV

For you, O Lord, have made me glad by your work; at the works of your hands I sing for joy.

How great are your works, O Lord! Your thoughts are very deep!

PSALM 92:4-5, NRSV

From Smith Wigglesworth:

Jesus Christ is the same yesterday, and today, and forever, and wants to manifest Himself to us in a similar way. It is His purpose that signs and wonders shall be seen in our midst, and men shall go away and declare, "We never saw it on this fashion."

God wants the gifts of healing and the working of miracles to be seen in our midst. In Acts 5:16 it says a multitude came out of the cities around Jerusalem, bringing sick folks and those vexed with unclean spirits, *and they were healed every one.* God wants us to move on into an experience where we see this happen.

—*Pressing Through*

You can trust God for a miracle.

Promises About Miracles

From the Bible:

Great are the works of the Lord, studied by all who delight in them.

Full of honor and majesty is his work, and his righteousness endures forever.

He has gained renown by his wonderful deeds; the Lord is gracious and merciful.

He has shown his people the power of his works, in giving them the heritage of the nations.

PSALM 111:2-4, 6, NRSV

How can we escape if we neglect so great a salvation? It was declared at first through the Lord, and it was attested to us by those who heard him, while God added his testimony by signs and wonders and various miracles, and by gifts of the Holy Spirit, distributed according to his will.

HEBREWS 2:3-4, NRSV

From Smith Wigglesworth:

May God take us on and on into this glorious fact of faith, that we may be so in the Holy Spirit that He will work the miraculous and prophetic through us.

And we will always know that it is no longer we but He who is working through us, bringing forth that which is in His own divine good pleasure.

—*The Gift of Prophecy*

You can trust God for a miracle.

Promises About Obedience

From the Bible:

See, I am setting before you today a blessing and a curse: the blessing, if you obey the commandments of the Lord your God that I am commanding you today; and the curse, if you do not obey the commandments of the Lord your God, but turn from the way that I am commanding you today, to follow other gods that you have not known.

Deuteronomy 11:26-28, NRSV

Be careful to obey all these words that I command you today, so that it may go well with you and with your children after you forever, because you will be doing what is good and right in the sight of the Lord your God.

Deuteronomy 12:28, NRSV

From Smith Wigglesworth:

The place of yieldedness is just where God wants us. People are saying, "I want the baptism, I want healing, I would like to know with certainty that I am a child of God." And I see nothing, absolutely nothing, in the way except unyieldedness to the plan of God. And that is what God wants from us: obedience.

When we begin yielding to God, He is able to fulfill His plan for our lives, and we come into that wonderful place where all we have to do is eat the fruits of Canaan.

But the thing God is looking for is obedience.

—*The Anointing of His Spirit*

God rewards your
obedience to Him.

Promises About Obedience

From the Bible:

And Samuel said, "Has the Lord as great delight in burnt offerings and sacrifices, as in obeying the voice of the Lord? Surely, to obey is better than sacrifice, and to heed than the fat of rams."

1 SAMUEL 15:22, NRSV

But this command I gave them, "Obey my voice, and I will be your God, and you shall be my people; and walk only in the way that I command you, so that it may be well with you."

JEREMIAH 7:23, NRSV

From Smith Wigglesworth:

When I will not do anything for myself, God will do something for me, and then I will gladly do anything for Him that He wants.

This is the purpose of the baptism of the Holy Spirit. It creates yielded and obedient men and women.

There is so much failure in self-assurance. We must never rest upon anything that is human. Our trust is in God, and God brings the victory. When we have no confidence in ourselves, then our whole trust rests upon the authority of the mighty God. He has promised to be with us at all times, and to make the path straight, and to make a way through the mountains.

—*Only Believe*

God rewards your
obedience to Him.

Promises About Obedience

From the Bible:

But he said, "Blessed rather are those who hear the word of God and obey it!"

LUKE 11:28, NRSV

Now by this we may be sure that we know him, if we obey his commandments.

Whoever says, "I have come to know him," but does not obey his commandments, is a liar, and in such a person the truth does not exist; but whoever obeys his word, truly in this person the love of God has reached perfection.

1 JOHN 2:3-5, NRSV

By this we know that we love the children of God, when we love God and obey his commandments.

For the love of God is this, that we obey his commandments. And his commandments are not burdensome.

1 JOHN 5:2-3, NRSV

From Smith Wigglesworth:

Are you willing that God shall have His way today?

Jesus said, "I will show him how great things he must suffer for my name's sake." But Paul saw that these things were working out a far more exceeding weight of glory. You who want a touch from God, are you willing to follow Him? Will you obey Him?

Beloved, all in the Father's house is ours, but it will come only through obedience. And when He can trust us, we will not come behind in anything.

—*The Anointing of the Spirit*

God rewards your
obedience to Him.

Promises About Perseverance

From the Bible:

No one shall be able to stand against you all the days of your life. As I was with Moses, so I will be with you; I will not fail you or forsake you.

Be strong and courageous; for you shall put this people in possession of the land that I swore to their ancestors to give them.

Only be strong and very courageous, being careful to act in accordance with all the law that my servant Moses commanded you; do not turn from it to the right hand or to the left, so that you may be successful wherever you go.

This book of the law shall not depart out of your mouth; you shall meditate on it day and night, so that you may be careful to act in accordance with all that is written in it. For then you shall make your way prosperous, and then you shall be successful.

JOSHUA 1:5-8, NRSV

From Smith Wigglesworth:

What makes us lose confidence is disobedience to God and His laws. Jesus said it was because of those who stood around that He prayed; He knew that God always heard Him. And because Jesus knew that His Father always heard Him, He knew that the dead could come forth.

At times there seems to be a stone wall in front of us. Everything seems black as midnight, and there is nothing left but confidence in God. There is no feeling.

We must have confidence to believe that He will not fail, indeed, cannot fail. We shall never get anywhere if we depend upon our feelings. There is something a thousand times better than feelings, and it is the naked Word of God.

—The Anointing of His Spirit

The Lord is your
strength to endure.

Promises About Perseverance

From the Bible:

Therefore, since we are justified by faith, we have peace with God through our Lord Jesus Christ, through whom we have obtained access to this grace in which we stand; and we boast in our hope of sharing the glory of God.

And not only that, but we also boast in our sufferings, knowing that suffering produces endurance, and endurance produces character, and character produces hope, and hope does not disappoint us, because God's love has been poured into our hearts through the Holy Spirit that has been given to us.

For while we were still weak, at the right time Christ died for the ungodly.

ROMANS 5:1-6, NRSV

From Smith Wigglesworth:

The trial of your faith is more precious than gold that perishes. And we must give all, yield all, as our Great Refiner puts us again and again in the melting pot.

What for? To lose the chaff, that the pure gold of His presence is so clearly seen and His glorious image reflected.

We must be steadfast until all His purposes are wrought out. We will not perish though we are tried by fire.

What is going to appear at the appearing of Jesus? Faith! Faith! The establishing of your heart by the grace of the Spirit, not to crush, but to refine; not to destroy, but to enlarge you.

—*Our Living Hope*

The Lord is your strength to endure.

Promises About Perseverance

From the Bible:

Therefore, my dear brothers, stand firm. Let nothing move you. Always give yourselves fully to the work of the Lord, because you know that your labor in the Lord is not in vain.

1 CORINTHIANS 15:58, NIV

So if you think you are standing, watch out that you do not fall.

No testing has overtaken you that is not common to everyone. God is faithful, and he will not let you be tested beyond your strength, but with the testing he will also provide the way out so that you may be able to endure it.

1 CORINTHIANS 10:12-13, NRSV

From Smith Wigglesworth:

God brings us to a place where there are difficulties, where there is no pleasure, where there are hard corners. We know there are no possibilities on the human side—God must do it.

All these places are of God's ordering—God must do it. God allows trials, difficulties, temptations, and perplexities to come along our path, but there is not a temptation or trial that comes to us but that He has a way out. We do not have a way out; it is God who can bring us through!

—*The Anointing of His Spirit*

The Lord is your
strength to endure.

Promises About Perseverance

From the Bible:

Consider him who endured such hostility against himself from sinners, so that you may not grow weary or lose heart.

In your struggle against sin you have not yet resisted to the point of shedding your blood.

And you have forgotten the exhortation that addresses you as children—"My child, do not regard lightly the discipline of the Lord, or lose heart when you are punished by him; for the Lord disciplines those whom he loves, and chastises every child whom he accepts."

HEBREWS 12:36, NRSV

From Smith Wigglesworth:

You will be sifted as wheat. You will be tried as though some strange thing happened to you. You will be put in places where you will have to put your whole trust in God.

There is no such thing as anyone being tried beyond what God will allow. Every trial is to bring you to a greater position in God. The trial that tries your faith will help you know that faith from God will be forthcoming in the next test.

No man is able to win victory save through the power of the risen Christ within him. You will never be able to say, "I did this or that." You will desire to give God the glory for everything.

—Our Risen Christ

The Lord is your strength to endure.

Promises About Perseverance

From the Bible:

My brothers and sisters, whenever you face trials of any kind, consider it nothing but joy, because you know that the testing of your faith produces endurance; and let endurance have its full effect, so that you may be mature and complete, lacking in nothing.

Blessed is anyone who endures temptation. Such a one has stood the test and will receive the crown of life that the Lord has promised to those who love him.

JAMES 1:2-4,12, NRSV

From Smith Wigglesworth:

If you are sure of your ground, if you are counting on the presence of the living Christ within, you can laugh when you see things getting worse. God would have you settled and grounded in Christ, and it is only as you are filled with the Holy Spirit that you become steadfast and unmovable in Him.

At the cross, Jesus offered Himself without spot to God. Then God led Him right through to the empty tomb, to the ascension glory, to a place on the throne. God will take us in like manner, and the Holy Spirit will lead us every step of the way. The Son of God will never be satisfied until we are with Him, sharing His glory and His throne.

—Our Risen Christ

The Lord is your strength to endure.

Promises About Power

From the Bible:

But you will receive power when the Holy Spirit has come upon you; and you will be my witnesses in Jerusalem, in all Judea and Samaria, and to the ends of the earth.

ACTS 1:8, NRSV

For Christ did not send me to baptize but to proclaim the gospel, and not with eloquent wisdom, so that the cross of Christ might not be emptied of its power.

For the message about the cross is foolishness to those who are perishing, but to us who are being saved it is the power of God.

1 CORINTHIANS 1:17-18, NRSV

From Smith Wigglesworth:

God wants to flow through you with measureless power of divine utterance and grace until you are a flame of spiritual fire. God intends each soul in Pentecost to be a live wire. Not a monument, but a movement. So many people have been baptized with the Holy Spirit; there was a movement, but they have become monuments and you cannot move them.

God, wake us out of sleep lest we should become indifferent to the glorious truth and the breath of the almighty power of God. We must be the light and salt of the earth, with the whole armor of God upon us.

—The Substance of Things Hoped For

You can receive power from on high.

Promises About Power

From the Bible:

My speech and my proclamation were not with plausible words of wisdom, but with a demonstration of the Spirit and of power, so that your faith might rest not on human wisdom but on the power of God.

1 CORINTHIANS 2:4-5, NRSV

For the kingdom of God depends not on talk but on power.

1 CORINTHIANS 4:20, NRSV

But we have this treasure in clay jars, so that it may be made clear that this extraordinary power belongs to God and does not come from us.

2 CORINTHIANS 4:7, NRSV

From Smith Wigglesworth:

For God has not accomplished something in us that should lie dormant, but He has brought within us a power, a revelation, a life that is so great that I believe God wants to reveal the greatness of it.

The possibilities of man in the hands of God! There isn't anything you can imagine greater than what that person may accomplish.

—*Christ in Us*

You can receive
power from on high.

Promises About Power

From the Bible:

He said to me, "My grace is sufficient for you, for power is made perfect in weakness." So, I will boast all the more gladly of my weaknesses, so that the power of Christ may dwell in me.

2 Corinthians 12:9, NRSV

For he was crucified in weakness, but lives by the power of God. For we are weak in him, but in dealing with you we will live with him by the power of God.

2 Corinthians 13:4, NRSV

From Smith Wigglesworth:

The Lord wants all saved people to receive power from on high—power to witness, power to act, power to show forth the divine manifestation of God within. The power of God will take you out of your own plans and put you into the plan of God.

You will be dismantled and divested of that which is purely of yourself and put into a divine order. The Lord will change you and put His mind where yours was, and thus enable you to have the mind of Christ.

Instead of your laboring according to your own plan, it will be God working in you to do His own good pleasure through the power of the Spirit within. Christ must reign within, which means the subjection of your will to make way for the working out of the good and acceptable and perfect will of God within.

—*Ye Shall Receive Power*

You can receive power from on high.

Promises About Power

From the Bible:

I pray that the God of our Lord Jesus Christ, the Father of glory, may give you a spirit of wisdom and revelation as you come to know him, so that, with the eyes of your heart enlightened, you may know what is the hope to which he has called you, what are the riches of his glorious inheritance among the saints, and what is the immeasurable greatness of his power for us who believe, according to the working of his great power.

God put this power to work in Christ when he raised him from the dead and seated him at his right hand in the heavenly places, far above all rule and authority and power and dominion, and above every name that is named, not only in this age but also in the age to come.

EPHESIANS 1:17-21, NRSV

From Smith Wigglesworth:

Everything that pertains to holiness and godliness; everything that denounces and brings to death the natural is always in the power of the risen Christ. And we have come into an endless power of a risen Christ.

We must be the mouthpiece of God, not by letter but by the Spirit. And we must be so in the will of God that He rejoices over us with singing. Isn't it lovely?

—*Ye Are Our Epistle*

You can receive
power from on high.

Promises About Power

From the Bible:

I want to know Christ and the power of his resurrection and the sharing of his sufferings by becoming like him in his death, if somehow I may attain the resurrection from the dead.

PHILIPPIANS 3:10-11, NRSV

Finally, be strong in the Lord and in the strength of his power.

Put on the whole armor of God, so that you may be able to stand against the wiles of the devil.

For our struggle is not against enemies of blood and flesh, but against the rulers, against the authorities, against the cosmic powers of this present darkness, against the spiritual forces of evil in the heavenly places.

EPHESIANS 6:10-12, NRSV

From Smith Wigglesworth:

There is life and power in the seed of the Word that is implanted within. There is more power in His Word than in any human objections. God's will for everyone is that we reign in life by Jesus Christ. We must come to see how wonderful we are in God and how helpless we are in ourselves.

God declared Himself more mighty than every opposing power when He cast out the power of darkness from heaven. The same power that cast Satan out of heaven dwells in everyone who is born of God. If you would realize this, you would reign in life.

—Ever Increasing Faith

You can receive power
from on high.

Promises About Praise

From the Bible:

You are enthroned as the Holy One; you are the praise of Israel.

PSALM 22:3, NIV

You have multiplied, O Lord my God, your wondrous deeds and your thoughts toward us; none can compare with you. Were I to proclaim and tell of them, they would be more than can be counted.

I have told the glad news of deliverance in the great congregation; see, I have not restrained my lips, as you know, O Lord.

I have not hidden your saving help within my heart, I have spoken of your faithfulness and your salvation; I have not concealed your steadfast love and your faithfulness from the great congregation.

PSALM 40:3-5, 9-10, NRSV

From Smith Wigglesworth:

Today we praise God for the fact that our glorious Jesus is the risen Christ. A church that doesn't know how to pray and shout will never be shaken. It is only when people have learned the secret of prayer, of power and of praise, that God comes forth.

Some people say, "Well, I praise God inwardly." But if there is an abundance of praise in our hearts, our mouths cannot help speaking it.

—*Ever Increasing Faith*

God dwells in the praise of His people.

Promises About Praise

From the Bible:

I will praise the name of God with a song; I will magnify him with thanksgiving.

This will please the Lord more than an ox or a bull with horns and hoofs.

PSALM 69:30-31, NRSV

But the hour is coming, and is now here, when the true worshipers will worship the Father in spirit and truth, for the Father seeks such as these to worship him.

God is spirit, and those who worship him must worship in spirit and truth.

JOHN 4:23-24, NRSV

And Mary said, "My soul magnifies the Lord, and my spirit rejoices in God my Savior, for he has looked with favor on the lowliness of his servant. Surely, from now on all generations will call me blessed; for the Mighty One has done great things for me, and holy is his name."

LUKE 1:46-49, NRSV

From Smith Wigglesworth:

The Holy Ghost is the One who magnifies the Lord Jesus Christ, the One who gives illumination of Him. If you're filled with the Holy Spirit, it is impossible to keep your tongue still.

We are filled with the Spirit in order that we may magnify the Lord, and in meetings the saints will glorify, magnify, praise, and worship the Lord in Spirit and in truth.

—The Gifts of the Spirit

God dwells in the praise
of His people.

Promises About Praise

From the Bible:

As he was now approaching the path down from the Mount of Olives, the whole multitude of the disciples began to praise God joyfully with a loud voice for all the deeds of power that they had seen, saying, "Blessed is the king who comes in the name of the Lord! Peace in heaven, and glory in the highest heaven!"

LUKE 19:37-38, NRSV

Through him, then, let us continually offer a sacrifice of praise to God, that is, the fruit of lips that confess his name.

Do not neglect to do good and to share what you have, for such sacrifices are pleasing to God.

HEBREWS 13:15-16, NRSV

From Smith Wigglesworth:

The praise cannot come out unless it is inside. There must first be the inner working of the power of God; it is He who changes the heart and transforms the life. Before there is any outward evidence there must be the inflow of divine life.

When people come and pray and praise as the early disciples did, there will be something doing. People who come will catch fire and want to come again. They will have no use for a place where everything has been formal, dry, and dead.

—Ever Increasing Faith

God dwells in the praise
of His people.

Promises About Prayer

From the Bible:

[Jesus said,] "Ask, and it will be given you; search, and you will find; knock, and the door will be opened for you.

"For everyone who asks receives, and everyone who searches finds, and for everyone who knocks, the door will be opened.

"Is there anyone among you who, if your child asks for bread, will give a stone?

"Or if the child asks for a fish, will give a snake?

"If you then, who are evil, know how to give good gifts to your children, how much more will your Father in heaven give good things to those who ask him!"

MATTHEW 7:7-11, NRSV

From Smith Wigglesworth:

We have the blessed assurance with God that if we ask anything according to His will, He hears us. And if we know that God hears us, whatever we ask, we know that we have the petitions we desire of Him.

Do you go to God for purity of heart? It is His will that you should receive it, and if you ask in faith, you can know you have the petition you desire of Him. Do you desire that the might of God's spirit shall accompany your ministry? That is according to the will of God.

Continue in the presence of our heavenly Father, quietly reminding Him that this is what you desire, and He will not fail to give you an exceeding abundance, above all ye ask or think.

—*The Anointing of His Spirit*

Ask and it will be given to you.

Promises About Prayer

From the Bible:

He was praying in a certain place, and after he had finished, one of his disciples said to him, "Lord, teach us to pray, as John taught his disciples."

He said to them, "When you pray, say: Father, hallowed be your name. Your kingdom come.

"Give us each day our daily bread.

"And forgive us our sins, for we ourselves forgive everyone indebted to us. And do not bring us to the time of trial."

LUKE 11:1-4, NRSV

[Jesus said,] "But I say to you that listen, love your enemies, do good to those who hate you, bless those who curse you, pray for those who abuse you."

LUKE 6:27-28, NRSV

From Smith Wigglesworth:

God has called us to loose the bonds of wickedness, undo the heavy burden, let the oppressed go free, and break the yokes that the devil has put upon them. Pray in faith.

Remember: Those who ask receive. Ask and it shall be given unto you. Live for God. Keep yourself clean and holy. Live under the unction of the Holy Spirit. Let the mind of Christ be yours so that you live in God's desires and plans.

—*The Anointing of the Spirit*

Ask and it will be given to you.

Promises About Prayer

From the Bible:

For in hope we were saved. Now hope that is seen is not hope. For who hopes for what is seen?

But if we hope for what we do not see, we wait for it with patience.

Likewise the Spirit helps us in our weakness; for we do not know how to pray as we ought, but that very Spirit intercedes with sighs too deep for words.

And God, who searches the heart, knows what is the mind of the Spirit, because the Spirit intercedes for the saints according to the will of God.

ROMANS 8:24-27, NRSV

From Smith Wigglesworth:

Who knows how to pray as the Spirit prays?

What kind of prayer does the Spirit pray? The Spirit always brings to remembrance the mind of the Scriptures and brings forth all your cry and your need better than your words. The Spirit takes the Word of God and brings your heart, mind, soul, cry, and need into the presence of God.

So we are not able to pray as the Spirit prays. The Spirit only prays according to the will of God, and the will of God is all in the Word of God. No man is able to speak according to the mind of God and bring forth the deep things of God out of his own mind.

—*Ye Are Our Epistle*

Ask and it will be given to you.

Promises About Righteousness

From the Bible:

And [Abraham] believed the Lord; and the Lord reckoned it to him as righteousness.

GENESIS 15:6, NRSV

The Lord rewards everyone for his righteousness and his faithfulness.

1 SAMUEL 26:23, NRSV

Lead me, O Lord, in your righteousness because of my enemies; make your way straight before me.

PSALM 5:8, NRSV

The Lord rewarded me according to my righteousness; according to the cleanness of my hands he recompensed me.

PSALM 18:20, NRSV

From Smith Wigglesworth:

It is the purpose of God that as we are indwelt by the Spirit of His Son, we should love righteousness and hate iniquity. There is a place for us in Christ Jesus where we are no longer under condemnation, but where the heavens are always open to us.

Abraham attained to the place where he became a friend of God. He believed God, and God counted that to him for righteousness. Righteousness was imputed to him.

—Ever Increasing Faith

You are the righteousness of Christ.

Promises About Righteousness

From the Bible:

As it is written: "There is no one righteous, not even one; there is no one who understands, no one who seeks God.

"All have turned away, they have become worthless; there is no one who does good, not even one."

Therefore no one will be declared righteous in his sight by observing the law; rather, through the law we become conscious of sin.

But now a righteousness from God, apart from law, has been made known, to which the Law and the Prophets testify.

ROMANS 3:10-12, 20-21, NIV

From Smith Wigglesworth:

In Jesus, God has not given you a pattern which is impossible to copy. Beloved, Jesus hated sin. If you have hatred for sin, you have something worth millions. Oh, the blood of Jesus Christ, God's Son, cleanses us from all sin.

I believe the hope of the church for the future is in its being purified—made like unto Jesus, pure in heart, pure in thought. Then, when a believer lays hands on the sick, Satan has no power; when he commands him to leave, Satan has to go.

—*Only Believe!*

You are the righteousness of Christ.

Promises About Righteousness

From the Bible:

But if Christ is in you, though the body is dead because of sin, the Spirit is life because of righteousness.

If the Spirit of him who raised Jesus from the dead dwells in you, he who raised Christ from the dead will give life to your mortal bodies also through his Spirit that dwells in you.

So then, brothers and sisters, we are debtors, not to the flesh, to live according to the flesh—for if you live according to the flesh, you will die; but if by the Spirit you put to death the deeds of the body, you will live.

ROMANS 8:10-13, NRSV

From Smith Wigglesworth:

There is no such thing as your having liberty in your body if there is any sin there. When righteousness is there, righteousness abounds. When Christ is in your heart, enthroning your life, and sin is dethroned, then righteousness abounds and the Holy Spirit has great liberty. This is one of the highest positions of character.

My, what triumphs of heights, of lengths, of depths, of breadths there are in this holy place!

Where is it? Right inside.

—*Preparation for the Rapture*

You are the righteousness of Christ.

Promises About Righteousness

From the Bible:

For our sake he made him to be sin who knew no sin, so that in him we might become the righteousness of God.

2 CORINTHIANS 5:21, NRSV

You were taught to put away your former way of life, your old self, corrupt and deluded by its lusts, and to be renewed in the spirit of your minds, and to clothe yourselves with the new self, created according to the likeness of God in true righteousness and holiness.

EPHESIANS 4:22-24, NRSV

From Smith Wigglesworth:

Purity is bold. Take, for instance, a little child. It will gaze straight into your eyes for as long as you like, without winking once. The more pure, the more bold.

I tell you, God wants to bring us into the divine purity of heart and life—that holy boldness. Not officiousness; not swelled-headedness; not self-righteousness; but a pure, holy, divine appointing by the One who will come in and live with you, defying the power of Satan, and standing you in a place of victory—overcoming the world.

—*Divine Life and Divine Health*

You are the righteousness of Christ.

Promises About Righteousness

From the Bible:

And this is my prayer, that your love may overflow more and more with knowledge and full insight to help you to determine what is best, so that in the day of Christ you may be pure and blameless, having produced the harvest of righteousness that comes through Jesus Christ for the glory and praise of God.

PHILIPPIANS 1:9-11, NRSV

Now, discipline always seems painful rather than pleasant at the time, but later it yields the peaceful fruit of righteousness to those who have been trained by it.

Therefore lift your drooping hands and strengthen your weak knees, and make straight paths for your feet, so that what is lame may not be put out of joint, but rather be healed.

HEBREWS 12:11-13, NRSV

From Smith Wigglesworth:

God's operations upon us may be painful, but the wise saint will remember that among those whom God chastens, it yields the peaceable fruit of righteousness.

Therefore, let Him do with you what seems good, for He has His hand upon you and He will not willingly take it off until He has performed the thing He knows you need.

So if He comes with chastisement, be ready for chastisement. If He comes with correction, be ready for correction. Whatever He wills to do, let Him do it and He will bring you to the land of plenty.

—About the Gifts of the Spirit

You are the righteousness of Christ.

Promises About Salvation

From the Bible:

I will give them one heart, and put a new spirit within them; I will remove the heart of stone from their flesh and give them a heart of flesh, so that they may follow my statutes and keep my ordinances and obey them. Then they shall be my people, and I will be their God.

EZEKIEL 11:19-20, NRSV

You have given me the shield of your salvation, and your help has made me great.

2 SAMUEL 22:36, NRSV

From Smith Wigglesworth:

God is gracious and not willing that any should perish. How many are willing to make a clean breast of their sins? I tell you that the moment you do this, God will open heaven.

It is an easy thing for Him to save your soul and heal your disease, if you will but come and shelter today in the secret place of the most High. He will satisfy you with long life and show you His salvation. In His presence is fullness of joy; at His right hand there are pleasures for evermore.

There is full redemption for all, through the precious blood of the Son of God.

—*The Words of This Life*

Jesus is your salvation
in life and eternity.

Promises About Salvation

From the Bible:

Jesus answered him, "Very truly, I tell you, no one can see the kingdom of God without being born from above."

Nicodemus said to him, "How can anyone be born after having grown old? Can one enter a second time into the mother's womb and be born?"

Jesus answered, "Very truly, I tell you, no one can enter the kingdom of God without being born of water and Spirit.

"What is born of the flesh is flesh, and what is born of the Spirit is spirit.

"Do not be astonished that I said to you, 'You must be born from above.'

"The wind blows where it chooses, and you hear the sound of it, but you do not know where it comes from or where it goes. So it is with everyone who is born of the Spirit."

JOHN 3:3-8, NRSV

From Smith Wigglesworth:

The new birth is a new life; it is regenerative. It is holy, it is divine, it is faith, it is Christ. And He is with you always, moving you, changing you, thrilling you, causing you to live in the glory. In a believing position.

The condition of salvation is not a pressure of saying that if you do not continually believe, you shall be lost. Faith is life. Life is presence, a presence of changing from one state of glory to another.

—Preparation for the
Second Coming of the Lord

Jesus is your salvation
in life and eternity.

Promises About Salvation

From the Bible:

There is salvation in no one else [but Jesus], for there is no other name under heaven given among mortals by which we must be saved.

ACTS 4:12, NRSV

As we work together with him, we urge you also not to accept the grace of God in vain.

For he says, "At an acceptable time I have listened to you, and on a day of salvation I have helped you." See, now is the acceptable time; see, now is the day of salvation!

2 CORINTHIANS 6:1-2, NRSV

From Smith Wigglesworth:

Saul was probably the greatest persecutor of the early Christians. He was on his way to Damascus for the purpose of destroying the church there.

How did God deal with such a one? He should have dealt with him in judgment. God dealt with him in mercy. Oh, the wondrous love of God! He loved the saints at Damascus, and the way He preserved them was through the salvation of the man who purposed to scatter and destroy them.

Our God delights to be merciful, and His grace is vouchsafed daily to both sinner and saint. He shows mercy to all.

—*Paul's Conversion and His Baptism*

Jesus is your salvation
in life and eternity.

Promises About Salvation

From the Bible:

Now I rejoice, not because you were grieved, but because your grief led to repentance; for you felt a godly grief, so that you were not harmed in any way by us.

For godly grief produces a repentance that leads to salvation and brings no regret, but worldly grief produces death.

2 CORINTHIANS 7:9-10, NRSV

Only, live your life in a manner worthy of the gospel of Christ, so that ... you are standing firm in one spirit, striving side by side with one mind for the faith of the gospel, and are in no way intimidated by your opponents. For them this is evidence of their destruction, but of your salvation. And this is God's doing.

PHILIPPIANS 1:27-28, NRSV

From Smith Wigglesworth:

The new birth—the new creation, the quickening, the being made after Him—is a very beautiful thing if you put it in this perfect order: When you are born of God, His nature comes in. We are conceived by the Word, quickened by the power, and made after His order. That which is from above has entered into that which is below, and you have become a quickened spirit.

You were dead, without spiritual aspiration, without desire. As soon as this comes in, aspiration, desire, and prayer ascend, lifting you higher and higher, and you have moved toward heavenly things. This is the most divine order you could have. This is the spiritual order—God manifested in the flesh, quickening us by the Spirit, making us like Him.

—Preparation for the
Second Coming of the Lord

Jesus is your salvation in life and eternity.

Promises About Salvation

From the Bible:

Therefore, my beloved, just as you have always obeyed me, not only in my presence, but much more now in my absence, work out your own salvation with fear and trembling; for it is God who is at work in you, enabling you both to will and to work for his good pleasure.

PHILIPPIANS 2:12-13, NRSV

But since we belong to the day, let us be sober, and put on the breastplate of faith and love, and for a helmet the hope of salvation.

1 THESSALONIANS 5:8, NRSV

From Smith Wigglesworth:

Did you believe before you were saved? So many people would be saved, but they want to feel saved first.

There was never a person who felt saved before he believed. God's plan is always this: If we will believe, God wants to bring us all to a definite place of unswerving faith and confidence in Himself.

Direct your desire toward God, and you will have desires from God. He will meet you on the lines of those desires when you reach out in simple faith.

—Ever Increasing Faith

Jesus is your salvation
in life and eternity.

Promises About the Second Coming

From the Bible:

[Jesus said,] "Do not let your hearts be troubled. Believe in God, believe also in me.

"In my Father's house there are many dwelling places. If it were not so, would I have told you that I go to prepare a place for you?

"And if I go and prepare a place for you, I will come again and will take you to myself, so that where I am, there you may be also. And you know the way to the place where I am going."

JOHN 14:1-4, NRSV

From Smith Wigglesworth:

Are you ready? What for? To believe the Scriptures about the Second Coming. That is necessary. The Scripture is our foundation to build upon properly. Christ is the cornerstone; we are all in the building.

Oh! If I could let you see that wonderful city coming down out of heaven, with countless numbers of citizens. A city coming down out of heaven with trillions of people making the city.

Get ready for that. Claim your rights in God's order. Do not give way. Have faith in God. Believe the Scripture is for you.

—*Workers Together with God*

Christ is preparing a heavenly home for you.

Promises About the Second Coming

From the Bible:

But our citizenship is in heaven. And we eagerly await a Savior from there, the Lord Jesus Christ, who, by the power that enables him to bring everything under his control, will transform our lowly bodies so that they will be like his glorious body.

Therefore, my brothers, you whom I love and long for, my joy and crown, that is how you should stand firm in the Lord, dear friends!

PHILIPPIANS 3:20–4:1, NIV

From Smith Wigglesworth:

Do you love His appearing? Or are you merely concerned with the data as to when He is to come, or the signs of His coming?

Those who love His appearing love Him. They love the thought of His appearing, love the thought of His being satisfied in His people, love the thought of His receiving His kingdom, love the thought of His enemies being subdued under Him.

Love His appearing. Why? Because He is lovely. Love the appearing of the lovely One who is to receive the consummation of His love, who loved His own even unto the end. He shall see of the travail of His soul and be satisfied.

—*The Gifts of Healing and
the Working of Miracles*

Christ is preparing a heavenly home for you.

Promises About the Second Coming

From the Bible:

Fight the good fight of the faith. Take hold of the eternal life to which you were called when you made your good confession in the presence of many witnesses.

In the sight of God, who gives life to everything, and of Christ Jesus, who while testifying before Pontius Pilate made the good confession, I charge you to keep this command without spot or blame until the appearing of our Lord Jesus Christ, which God will bring about in his own time—God, the blessed and only Ruler, the King of kings and Lord of lords, who alone is immortal and who lives in unapproachable light, whom no one has seen or can see. To him be honor and might forever. Amen.

1 TIMOTHY 6:12-16, NIV

From Smith Wigglesworth:

I feel sometimes that we have just as much as we can digest, yet there are such divine nuggets of precious truth held before our hearts, it makes us understand there are yet heights, and depths, and lengths, and breadths of the knowledge of God laid up for us in heaven.

We might truly say,

"My heavenly bank, my heavenly bank,

"The house of God's treasure and store.

"I have plenty in here; I'm a real millionaire."

Glory! Never to be poverty-struck any more, having an inward knowledge of a greater bank in heaven than anyone has ever known about. It is stored up, nugget upon nugget, weights of glory, expressions of the invisible Christ to be seen by men.

—*Glory and Virtue*

Christ is preparing a heavenly home for you.

Promises About the Second Coming

From the Bible:

Blessed be the God and Father of our Lord Jesus Christ! By his great mercy he has given us a new birth into a living hope through the resurrection of Jesus Christ from the dead, and into an inheritance that is imperishable, undefiled, and unfading, kept in heaven for you, who are being protected by the power of God through faith for a salvation ready to be revealed in the last time.

In this you rejoice, even if now for a little while you have had to suffer various trials, so that the genuineness of your faith—being more precious than gold that, though perishable, is tested by fire—may be found to result in praise and glory and honor when Jesus Christ is revealed.

1 PETER 1:3-7, NRSV

From Smith Wigglesworth:

Lively hope is leaving everything behind you.

Lively hope is keeping the vision.

Lively hope sees Him coming!

Lively hope, we live in it! We are not trying to make ourselves feel that we believe. The lively hope is ready, waiting, filled with the joy and expectation of the King. Praise the Lord!

If you have any love for the world you cannot have this hope, because Jesus is not coming for the world. He is coming to the heavenlies, and all the heavenlies are going to Him. There is nothing but joy there!

—*Smith Wigglesworth:*
A Man Who Walked with God

Christ is preparing a heavenly home for you.

Promises About Service

From the Bible:

For we are God's fellow workers; you are God's field, God's building.

Unlike so many, we do not peddle the word of God for profit. On the contrary, in Christ we speak before God with sincerity, like men sent from God.

By the grace God has given me, I laid a foundation as an expert builder, and someone else is building on it. But each one should be careful how he builds.

For no one can lay any foundation other than the one already laid, which is Jesus Christ.

If any man builds on this foundation using gold, silver, costly stones, wood, hay or straw, his work will be shown for what it is, because the Day will bring it to light. It will be revealed with fire, and the fire will test the quality of each man's work.

1 CORINTHIANS 3:9-13, NIV

From Smith Wigglesworth:

Never try to get the applause of the people by any natural thing. Yours is a spiritual work. Yours has to be a spiritual breath. Your word has to be the Word of God. Your counsel cannot be for personal gain.

You have to have such solid, holy reverence on every line so when you handle anybody you handle them for God, and you handle the church as the Church of God.

As the church is bound together in one Spirit, it grows into the temple of the Lord, and it has one voice, one desire, and one plan. And when we want souls saved we are all of one mind.

—*Our Calling*

There is joy in serving Jesus.

Promises About Service

From the Bible:

Have nothing to do with profane myths and old wives' tales. Train yourself in godliness, for, while physical training is of some value, godliness is valuable in every way, holding promise for both the present life and the life to come.

The saying is sure and worthy of full acceptance.

For to this end we toil and struggle, because we have our hope set on the living God, who is the Savior of all people, especially of those who believe.

1 TIMOTHY 4:7-10, NRSV

For the grace of God has appeared, bringing salvation to all, training us to renounce impiety and worldly passions, and in the present age to live lives that are self-controlled, upright, and godly.

TITUS 2:11-12, NRSV

From Smith Wigglesworth:

The obedient always obey God when He first speaks. It is the people of God that He will use to make the world know that there is a God.

The just shall live by faith. You cannot talk about things which you have never experienced. It seems to me that God has a process of training us. You cannot take people into the depth of God unless you have been broken yourself. I have been broken and broken and broken.

Praise God that He is near to them that are of a broken heart. You must have a brokenness to get into the depths of God.

—*The Confidence That We Have in Him*

There is joy in serving Jesus.

Promises About Service

From the Bible:

Whoever wishes to be great among you must be your servant, and whoever wishes to be first among you must be your slave; just as the Son of Man came not to be served but to serve, and to give his life a ransom for many.

MATTHEW 20:26-28, NRSV

We must work the works of him who sent me while it is day; night is coming when no one can work.

JOHN 9:4, NRSV

From Smith Wigglesworth:

If God lays hold of you by the Spirit, you will find that there is an end of everything and a beginning of God, so that your whole being becomes seasoned with a divine likeness to God.

He will begin not only to use you, but He has taken you in hand, so that you might be a vessel of honor. And our lives are not to be for ourselves, for if we live unto ourselves, we shall die. But if we, through the Spirit, do mortify the evils of the body, we shall live.

In this place of death we are subject to the powers of God, but he that liveth to himself shall die. The man in the former place lives a life of freedom and joy and blessing and service, and a life which brings blessing to others.

—Divine Life Brings Divine Health

There is joy in serving Jesus.

Promises About Service

From the Bible:

For God is not unjust; he will not overlook your work and the love that you showed for his sake in serving the saints, as you still do.

And we want each one of you to show the same diligence so as to realize the full assurance of hope to the very end, so that you may not become sluggish, but imitators of those who through faith and patience inherit the promises.

When God made a promise to Abraham, because he had no one greater by whom to swear, he swore by himself, saying, "I will surely bless you and multiply you."

And thus Abraham, having patiently endured, obtained the promise.

HEBREWS 6:10-15, NRSV

From Smith Wigglesworth:

To be persecuted for Christ's sake is to be joined up with a blessed, blessed people. But, better still, it means to be united with our Lord Jesus in the closest of fellowship, the fellowship of His suffering. There is a day coming when we will rejoice greatly that we have been privileged to suffer for His name's sake.

Beloved, God wants witnesses—witnesses to the truth, witnesses to the fullness of redemption. He wants deliverance from sin and disease by the eternal power working in them, as they are filled with life through the Spirit.

God wants us to believe that we may be ministers of that kind—of glorious things wrought in us by the Holy Spirit.

—*Keeping the Vision*

There is joy in serving Jesus.

Promises About Spiritual Gifts

From the Bible:

Now we have received not the spirit of the world, but the Spirit that is from God, so that we may understand the gifts bestowed on us by God.

And we speak of these things in words not taught by human wisdom but taught by the Spirit, interpreting spiritual things to those who are spiritual.

Those who are unspiritual do not receive the gifts of God's Spirit, for they are foolishness to them, and they are unable to understand them because they are spiritually discerned.

Those who are spiritual discern all things, and they are themselves subject to no one else's scrutiny.

"For who has known the mind of the Lord so as to instruct him?" But we have the mind of Christ.

1 CORINTHIANS 2:12-16, NRSV

From Smith Wigglesworth:

God has privileged us in Christ Jesus to live above the ordinary plane of life. Those who want to be "ordinary" and live on a lower plane can do so. But as for me, I will not!

The same unction, the same zeal, the same Holy Spirit power is at our command as was at the command of Stephen and the apostles. We have the same God that Abraham had, that Elijah had, and we need not come behind in any gift or grace.

We may not possess the gifts as abiding gifts, but as we are full of the Spirit, it is possible, when there is a need, for God to manifest every gift of the Spirit through us—a manifestation of the gifts as God may choose to use us.

—Extraordinary

God has given you
gifts of the Spirit.

Promises About Spiritual Gifts

From the Bible:

Now there are varieties of gifts, but the same Spirit; and there are varieties of services, but the same Lord; and there are varieties of activities, but it is the same God who activates all of them in everyone.

To each is given the manifestation of the Spirit for the common good.

To one is given through the Spirit the utterance of wisdom, and to another the utterance of knowledge according to the same Spirit, to another faith by the same Spirit, to another gifts of healing by the one Spirit, to another the working of miracles, to another prophecy, to another the discernment of spirits, to another various kinds of tongues, to another the interpretation of tongues.

All these are activated by one and the same Spirit, who allots to each one individually just as the Spirit chooses.

1 CORINTHIANS 12:4-11, NRSV

From Smith Wigglesworth:

It is not right to think that because you have a gift you are to wave it before the people and try to get their minds upon that. If you do, you will be out of the will of God.

Gifts and calling are given by God, but remember that He calls you to account for the gifts being properly administered in a spiritual way after you have received it. It is not given to adorn you, but to sustain, build, edify, and bless the church.

When the church receives this edification, and God ministers through that member, then all of the members will rejoice together. God moves upon us as His offspring, as His choice, and fruit of the earth.

—*About the Gifts of the Spirit*

God has given you
gifts of the Spirit.

Promises About Spiritual Gifts

From the Bible:

For just as the body is one and has many members, and all the members of the body, though many, are one body, so it is with Christ.

For in the one Spirit we were all baptized into one body—Jews or Greeks, slaves or free—and we were all made to drink of one Spirit.

Indeed, the body does not consist of one member but of many.

If the foot would say, "Because I am not a hand, I do not belong to the body," that would not make it any less a part of the body.

And if the ear would say, "Because I am not an eye, I do not belong to the body," that would not make it any less a part of the body.

If the whole body were an eye, where would the hearing be? If the whole body were hearing, where would the sense of smell be?

But as it is, God arranged the members in the body, each one of them, as he chose.

1 Corinthians 12:12-18, NRSV

From Smith Wigglesworth:

There is a great weakness in the Body of Christ because of ignorance concerning the Spirit of God and His gifts. God would have us know His will concerning the power and manifestation of His Spirit. He would have us ever hungry to receive more of His Spirit.

Now there are diversities of gifts, but the same Spirit. Every manifestation of the Spirit is given that we might profit. When the Holy Spirit is moving in an assembly, and His gifts are in operation, everyone will profit.

—*Ever Increasing Faith*

God has given you
gifts of the Spirit.

Promises About Spiritual Gifts

From the Bible:

Now you are the body of Christ and individually members of it.

And God has appointed in the church first apostles, second prophets, third teachers; then deeds of power, then gifts of healing, forms of assistance, forms of leadership, various kinds of tongues.

Are all apostles? Are all prophets? Are all teachers? Do all work miracles?

Do all possess gifts of healing? Do all speak in tongues? Do all interpret?

But strive for the greater gifts. And I will show you a still more excellent way.

1 CORINTHIANS 12:27-31, NRSV

From Smith Wigglesworth:

While it is right to covet earnestly the best gifts, you must recognize that the all-important thing is to be filled with the power of the Holy Spirit. You will not have trouble with people who are filled with the power of the Holy Spirit, but you will have a lot of trouble with people who have the gifts and have no power.

The Lord wants us to be so filled with the Holy Spirit that it will be the Holy Spirit manifesting Himself through the gifts. Where the glory of God alone is desired we can look for every needed gift to be made manifest. To glorify God is better than to idolize gifts.

—*Ever Increasing Faith*

God has given you gifts of the Spirit.

Promises About Spiritual Gifts

From the Bible:

The end of all things is near; therefore be serious and discipline yourselves for the sake of your prayers.

Above all, maintain constant love for one another, for love covers a multitude of sins.

Be hospitable to one another without complaining.

Like good stewards of the manifold grace of God, serve one another with whatever gift each of you has received.

Whoever speaks must do so as one speaking the very words of God; whoever serves must do so with the strength that God supplies, so that God may be glorified in all things through Jesus Christ. To him belong the glory and the power forever and ever. Amen.

1 Peter 4:7-11, NRSV

From Smith Wigglesworth:

You are to have the gifts and claim them, and the Lord will certainly change your life, and you will be new men and women.

Are you asking for a double portion? I trust that no one shall come behind in any gift. You may say, "I have asked. Do you think God will be pleased to have me ask again?"

Yea, go before Him. Ask again, and it shall be no longer "I," but the Holy Spirit who operates, and we shall see and know His power because we believe.

—*Spiritual Gifts*

> God has given you
> gifts of the Spirit.

Promises About Victory

From the Bible:

The Lord answer you in the day of trouble! The name of the God of Jacob protect you!

May he send you help from the sanctuary, and give you support from Zion.

May he remember all your offerings, and regard with favor your burnt sacrifices.

May he grant you your heart's desire, and fulfill all your plans.

May we shout for joy over your victory, and in the name of our God set up our banners. May the Lord fulfill all your petitions.

Now I know that the Lord will help his anointed; he will answer him from his holy heaven with mighty victories by his right hand.

Some take pride in chariots, and some in horses, but our pride is in the name of the Lord our God.

They will collapse and fall, but we shall rise and stand upright.

Give victory to the king, O Lord; answer us when we call.

PSALM 20, NRSV

From Smith Wigglesworth:

I always say you cannot sing victory in a minor key. And you never can have a spiritual horizon on a low note.

If your life isn't constant pitch you will never ring the bells of heaven. You must be in tune with God, and then the music will come out as sweet as possible.

—*Ye Are Our Epistle*

God will lead you to victory.

Promises About Victory

From the Bible:

O God, you have rejected us, broken our defenses;
you have been angry; now restore us!

You have caused the land to quake; you have
torn it open; repair the cracks in it, for it is totter-
ing.

You have made your people suffer hard things;
you have given us wine to drink that made us reel.

You have set up a banner for those who fear
you, to rally to it out of bowshot.

Give victory with your right hand, and answer
us, so that those whom you love may be rescued.

PSALM 60:1-5, NRSV

From Smith Wigglesworth:

You must never let go. Whatever you are seeking— a fresh revelation, light on the path, some particular thing—never let go. Victory is yours if you are earnest enough.

If you are in darkness, if you need a fresh revelation, if your mind needs relief, if there are problems you cannot solve, lay hold of God.

The divine power can only come when there is an end of our own self-sufficiency. But when we are broken, we must hold fast.

—*How to Be Transformed*

God will lead you to victory.

Promises About Victory

From the Bible:

For this perishable body must put on imperishability, and this mortal body must put on immortality.

When this perishable body puts on imperishability, and this mortal body puts on immortality, then the saying that is written will be fulfilled: "Death has been swallowed up in victory.

"Where, O death, is your victory? Where, O death, is your sting?"

The sting of death is sin, and the power of sin is the law.

But thanks be to God, who gives us the victory through our Lord Jesus Christ.

Therefore, my beloved, be steadfast, immovable, always excelling in the work of the Lord, because you know that in the Lord your labor is not in vain.

1 CORINTHIANS 15:53-58, NRSV

From Smith Wigglesworth:

As we enter into the divine, we will find sin dethroned; death has lost its sting, and victory is in Christ Jesus.

How? Reigning in life in Christ Jesus.

To reign in life means that you are over human weakness. To reign means you are on the rock, and everything else is under your feet.

Jesus has made for us a place of victory, that we may reign as kings over our bodies and over all thoughts of evil.

—Faith and Prayer

God will lead you to victory.

Promises About Victory

From the Bible:

Rejoice in the Lord always; again I will say, Rejoice.

Let your gentleness be known to everyone. The Lord is near.

Do not worry about anything, but in everything by prayer and supplication with thanksgiving let your requests be made known to God.

And the peace of God, which surpasses all understanding, will guard your hearts and your minds in Christ Jesus.

Finally, beloved, whatever is true, whatever is honorable, whatever is just, whatever is pure, whatever is pleasing, whatever is commendable, if there is any excellence and if there is anything worthy of praise, think about these things.

Keep on doing the things that you have learned and received and heard and seen in me, and the God of peace will be with you.

PHILIPPIANS 4:4-9, NRSV

From Smith Wigglesworth:

Do you see how Jesus mastered the devil in the wilderness? He knew He was the Son of God, and Satan came along with an "if."

How many times has Satan come to you this way? He says, "After all, you may be deceived. You know you really are not a child of God."

The devil knows if he can capture your thought life, he has won a victory over you. His great business is injecting thoughts, but if you are pure and holy you will shrink from them. God wants us to let the mind of Christ, that pure, holy, humble mind of Christ be in us.

—*Deliverance to the Captives*

God will lead you to victory.

Promises About Victory

From the Bible:

Everyone who believes that Jesus is the Christ has been born of God, and everyone who loves the parent loves the child.

By this we know that we love the children of God, when we love God and obey his commandments.

For the love of God is this, that we obey his commandments. And his commandments are not burdensome, for whatever is born of God conquers the world. And this is the victory that conquers the world, our faith.

Who is it that conquers the world but the one who believes that Jesus is the Son of God?

1 JOHN 5:1-5, NRSV

From Smith Wigglesworth:

If you are begotten by the incorruptible Word, which lives and abides forever, you know that within you is this living, definite hope, greater than yourself, more powerful than any dynamic force in the world.

With the audacity of faith we should throw ourselves into the omnipotence of God's divine plan. It is possible for the power of God to be so manifest in your human life that you will never be as you were before. You will be ever going forward, from victory to victory.

—*Dare to Believe*

God will lead you to victory.

About Smith Wigglesworth

Smith Wigglesworth (1859-1947) was a Pentecostal phenomenon, an ordinary Englishman used as a vessel for God's supernatural power. The legendary plumber turned preacher cast out demons, healed the sick, and stirred up a passion for God in the hearts of thousands.

His life and sermons have been captured in books such as *The Anointing of His Spirit, Ever Increasing Faith*, and *Faith That Prevails*. The Wigglesworth quotes in this book draw from published articles of his sermons and are lightly edited for today's readers.